COVENANT,

CONFLICT &

SALVATION IN

THE END-TIMES

The Redemption of Israel and the Nations

BARUCH BATTELSTEIN

DESTINY IMAGE EUROPE™ **srl**
Via Maiella, 1
66020 San Giovanni Teatino (Ch) - Italy

ISBN 13: 978-88-89127-45-2

For Worldwide Distribution, Printed in the U.S.A

1 2 3 4 5 6 7 8/10 09 08 07

This book and all other Destiny Image Europe™ books are available at bookstores and distributors worldwide.

To order products, or for any other correspondence:

DESTINY IMAGE EUROPE™ **srl**
Via Acquacorrente, 6
65123 - Pescara - Italy
Tel. +39 085 4716623 - Fax: +39 085 4716622
E-mail: info@eurodestinyimage.com

Or reach us on the Internet:
www.eurodestinyimage.com

CONTENTS

PROLOGUE

The secret of the Lord is with those who fear Him, and
His covenant is to let them know [it] (Psalm 25:14).

Many people have asked the question "What is it that G-d
wants from us?"

The key words in the verse above are "those who fear Him"
and "covenant." Again, those who fear Him will know His
covenant. These two phrases, "fear of the Lord" and "His
covenant" are inextricably linked. Here the concept of fear
means to revere, to be in awe of, to humble oneself before, or
to bring oneself into obedience to Him who is revered.

The first mention of the word *covenant* in the Tanach is in
Genesis 6:18 and 9:9–17, when G-d promises to establish a
covenant with Noah after the Flood, "between Me and between you and between every living creature among all flesh,"
a promise was made that "never again will all flesh be cut off
by the flood waters and never again will I destroy the earth
with a flood." This everlasting covenant was made with all the
earth's future populations in mind, and it is still in effect today,

symbolized by the beautiful rainbow arching through the sky after a rain.

We see that in Chapters 6 and 7 of Genesis G-d called Noah "a righteous man, perfect in his generations" and G-d said that Noah walked with Him.

One thing we know about Noah is that he "feared" G-d and revered Him. We know that when G-d told Noah to build the ark, "Noah did; according to all that G-d commanded him, so he did."

So it was that without ever having seen or known of rain prior to the flood, Noah was obedient and continued building the ark over many years in the face of the cruel mocking and laughing of his fellow man. He believed and "feared" G-d and was obedient. We all know the rest of this story.

And G-d, in His faithfulness, made a covenant with Noah and revealed it to him.

The next time the word covenant is seen in the Tanach is in Genesis 15:9–10 and 17–21 in connection with the promise that G-d made with Abram and his descendants concerning the land that G-d showed him[1] "from the river of Egypt to the great river, the river Euphrates."

This covenant was different from the one made with Noah in that an animal sacrifice of a heifer, goat, ram (cut in two), turtledove, and pigeon (being left whole) were brought before the Lord G-d, as He had instructed Abram. Then a smoking furnace and a firebrand passed between the pieces of the animals when the sun went down and it was dark. This was a blood covenant appointed by G-d and made with Abram.

There are so many verses from the Tanach that tell us clearly and precisely what G-d wants from us, and interestingly they all say the same thing. G-d is a covenant-making G-d. He desires fellowship with us, as He had with Adam and Eve in the Garden of Eden before sin entered into the picture.

G-d established and confirmed His covenant with Abram regarding the land, declaring,

"And I will place My covenant between Me and between you, and I will multiply you very greatly." And Abram fell upon his face, and G-d spoke with him, saying, "As for Me, behold My covenant is with you, and you shall become the father of a multitude of nations. And your name shall no longer be called Abram, but your name shall be Abraham, for I have made you the father of a multitude of nations. And I will make you exceedingly fruitful, and I will make you into nations, and kings will emerge from you. And I will establish My covenant between Me and between you and between your seed after you throughout their generations as an everlasting covenant, to be to you for a G-d and to your seed after you. And I will give you and your seed after you the land of your sojournings, the entire land of Canaan for an everlasting possession, and I will be to them for a G-d" (Genesis 17:2–8).

This covenant was everlasting, and not one word of it was dependent upon the faithfulness of Abraham or his descendants; instead, it rested entirely upon the faithfulness of the G-d of Israel. It was at this time that G-d changed the name of Abram to Abraham.

This covenant made between G-d and Abraham and his descendants required that every male among Abraham's clan be circumcised.[2] Thus, this covenant too was made with a blood sacrifice.

What does all this have to do with the words written within these pages? Because G-d is sovereign, He does not change,[3] and the word of the Lord is upright (that is, He cannot lie), and all His deeds are done with faith.[4] We can therefore be assured that it remains His plan and only His plan that is being made manifest here on earth[5] in order to bring about the fulfillment of yet another covenant. This covenant concerns the final redemption of His people, written about in Isaiah, Jeremiah, and Ezekiel, as well as many of the other books of the Tanach. This covenant will be made with His people, known as the descendants of Abraham, Isaac, and Jacob, and also known in the Tanach by other names and titles, such as the Hebrews, the Israelites, the sons of Israel, His chosen ones, the holy ones of Israel, and the Jews.

However, there is much written in the Tanach about the latter days, of the present age leading up to the final redemption of His people. It is a time known as, "Jacob's distress" or "Jacob's trouble."

> *For so said the Lord: A sound of quaking we have heard, fear, and there is no peace. Ask now and see whether a male gives birth. Why have I seen every man [with] his hands on his loins like a woman in confinement, and every face has turned to pallor? Ho! For that day is great, with none like it, and it is a time of distress for Jacob, through which he shall be saved* (Jeremiah 30:5–7).

We are told in Ezekiel exactly what, where, and how the Lord will bring this about.

> *But what enters your mind shall not come about, what you say, "Let us be like the nations, like the families of the lands, to serve wood and stone." As I live, says the Lord G-d, surely with a strong hand and with an outstretched arm and with poured out fury, will I reign over you. And I shall take you out of the peoples, and I shall gather you from the lands in which you were scattered, with a strong hand and with an outstretched arm and with poured out fury. And I shall bring you to the wilderness of the peoples, and I shall contend with you there face to face. As I contended with your forefathers in he wilderness of the land of Egypt, so will I contend with you, says the Lord G-d. And I shall cause you to pass under the rod, and I shall bring you into the transmission of the covenant* (Ezekiel 20:32–37).

G-d is faithful, merciful, gracious, and full of loving kindness. G-d knew from the beginning that He would execute His plan to redeem His people from the sin that had entered into the heart of man in the Garden of Eden. Thus, since that time,

He has been supernaturally working out His plan. However, He has indicated that there will come a time when He no longer will strive with man.[6] We can rejoice because it is clear that the plan He set forth in the Tanach to bring about the final redemption of His people is nearing completion.

During the years since 1948, the year G-d made Israel a nation once again upon the land that He had promised to the forefathers of faith and their descendants, the descendants of Abraham, Isaac, and Jacob, the prophetic clock of G-d is hastening toward the final fulfillment of all that He has written in His word regarding His sovereign plan of redemption for His chosen people.

Now we are about to enter into that time of "Jacob's distress," a time of great evil and much violence and suffering, yet through which G-d's chosen and faithful will be saved.

The revelation that this book will bring about for all those humble ones who love the Lord G-d, the Holy One of Israel, will indeed draw the reader closer to Him than ever before. Conversely, if you are one of His, yet you continue to demonstrate an arrogant spirit and a heart full of pride and iniquity, the words of the Lord in this book will break your spirit and give you a contrite heart, causing you to cry out to the living G-d as did David and Isaiah.

David heard the words of truth from Nathan regarding the sin and iniquity he was holding in his heart. Isaiah saw the reality of his sin with his own eyes in the presence of the Lord. So David through his ears and Isaiah with his eyes both recognized and confessed their sin, which produced a broken spirit and contrite heart within each man.

> *When Nathan the prophet came to him when he went to Bath-sheba. Be gracious to me, O G-d, according to Your kindness; according to Your great mercies, erase my transgressions. Wash me thoroughly of my iniquity, and purify me of my sin....Create for me a pure heart, O G-d, and renew a steadfast spirit within me. Do not cast me away from before You, and do not take Your holy*

spirit from me. Restore to me the joy of Your salvation, and let a noble spirit support me.... The sacrifices of G-d are a broken spirit; O G-d, You will not despise a broken and crushed heart (Psalm 51:2–4, 12–14, 19).

And I said, "Woe is me for I am lost, for I am a man of unclean lips, and amidst a people of unclean lips I dwell, for the King, the Lord of Hosts have my eyes seen." And one of the seraphim flew to me, and in his hand was a glowing coal; with tongs he had taken it from upon the altar. And he caused it to touch my mouth, and he said, "Behold, this has touched your lips; and your iniquity shall be removed, and your sin shall be atoned for" (Isaiah 6:5–7).

In these times, those who love the Lord G-d—who cry out to Him, call upon His name, and dwell in the shadow of the Almighty—will be shown His salvation.

He who dwells in the covert of the Most High will lodge in the shadow of the Almighty.
I shall say of the Lord [that He is] *my shelter and my fortress, my G-d in Whom I trust.*
For He will save you from the snare that traps from the devastating pestilence.
With His wing He will cover you, and under His wings you will take refuge; His truth is an encompassing shield.
You will not fear the fright of night, the arrow that flies by day; pestilence that prowls in darkness, destruction that ravages at noon.
A thousand will be stationed at your side, and ten thousand at your right hand; but it will not approach you.
You will but gaze with your eyes, and you will see the annihilation of the wicked.
For you [said], *"The Lord is my refuge"; the Most High you made your dwelling.*
No harm will befall you, nor will a plague draw near to your tent.
For He will command His angels on your behalf to guard you in all your ways.

On [their] *hands they will bear you, lest your foot stumble on a stone.*
On a young lion and a cobra you will tread; you will trample the young lion and the serpent.
For he yearns for Me, and I shall rescue him; I shall fortify him because he knows My name.
He will call Me and I shall answer him; I am with him in distress; I shall rescue him and I shall honor him.
With length of days I shall satiate him, and I shall show him My salvation (Psalm 91).

G-d wants to redeem us and show us His salvation. First, we must repent of our sin, cry out to Him, and return to Him. For many, I fear, this will mean great sorrow and pain before they come to that special place of humility and brokenness before the Lord. This has been the history of His people, and this seems to have never changed over the centuries.

Will you be one of His forgiven, the saved and redeemed ones of Israel?

ENDNOTES

1. Genesis 13:14–15.

2. Genesis 17:10–11.

3. Malachi 3:6.

4. Psalm 33:4.

5. Psalm 33:10–11.

6. Psalm 103:9.

Chapter One

THE COMING OF THE MESSIAH

All peoples, nations, and tongues shall serve him; his dominion is an eternal dominion, which will not be removed, and his kingdom is one which will not be destroyed (Daniel 7:14).

Today many people in Israel are looking and waiting for the Messiah to come. We must therefore examine and seek to understand Daniel's prophetic word regarding the coming of the Lord's Messiah and the establishment of the kingdom of G-d upon the earth.

In his vision we find Daniel literally standing before the throne of G-d in Heaven, where he sees the Ancient of Days is seated.

THE ANCIENT OF DAYS REIGNS

I was looking until thrones were set up, and the Ancient of Days sat; His raiment was as white as snow, and the hair of His head was like clean wool; His throne was sparks of fire, its wheels were a burning fire. A river of fire was flowing and emerging from before Him; a thousand thousands served Him, and ten thousand ten thousands arose before Him. Justice was established, and the books were opened (Daniel 7:9–10).

In these prophetic verses, Daniel describes the Lord G-d of Israel sitting on His throne in Heaven. The hair of His head was like pure wool, and His throne was ablaze with flames, its wheels were a burning fire.

Daniel actually saw the Lord seated on His throne in Heaven, and though it was ablaze with flames, it did not burn up nor did it harm Him. Daniel says a river of fire was flowing out before Him, and thousands upon thousands were attending Him and tens of thousands arose before Him.

THE COURT IS SET

Justice was established, and the books were opened. I saw then from the sound of the arrogant words that the horn spoke, I looked until the beast was slain, and its body was destroyed and given to a flame of fire. But as for the other beasts, their dominion was removed, and they were given an extension of life until a set time (Daniel 7:10c-12).

Interestingly, just as in court proceedings, the books are opened with the list of charges read as the defendant stands before the judge. In the midst of all this, Daniel could still hear the boastful words of the horn (beast) who was speaking out against G-d and His holy people.

Who is the beast? He is the one coming, empowered by "the serpent of old" and described earlier in the book of Daniel; he will be the political leader, the ruler over the revived Roman Empire or the Fourth Kingdom, represented by the feet and toes in Daniel's vision.

And what you saw, the feet and the toes—which were partly of potter's clay and partly of iron—so it will be a divided kingdom, and in it will be some of the strength of iron, in view of what you saw iron mixed with clay. And the toes of the feet were partly iron and partly clay, for part of the kingdom will be strong and part of it will be broken (Daniel 2:41–42).

Then I wished to determine the truth of the fourth beast, which was different from all of them—excessively dreadful;...And concerning the ten horns that were on its head, and the other one that came up and [the] *three* [that] *fell before it, and the horn that was like this and that had eyes and a mouth speaking arrogantly, and its appearance was greater than* [that of] *its companions. I looked and the horn that was like this waged war with the holy ones and overwhelmed them* (Daniel 7:19a, 20–21).

So he said, "The fourth beast [represents] *a fourth kingdom* [that] *will be on the earth, which will be different from all the kingdoms, and it will devour the whole land and trample it and crush it. And the ten horns that* [sprout] *from that kingdom* [represent] *ten kings* [that] *will rise, and the last one will rise after them, and he will be different from the first, and he will humble three kings"* (Daniel 7:23–24).

This political leader will speak out monstrous things against the Most High G-d of Israel.

And he will speak words against the Most High, and he will oppress the high holy ones, and he will think to change the times and the law, and they will be delivered into his hand until a time, two times, and half a time (Daniel 7:25).

His kingdom will be different from all other kingdoms that have ever come upon the earth, as it will "devour the whole earth and tread it down and crush it." For three and a half years (time, two times, and half a time) no one will be able to stand against this political leader as he will devour, tread down, and crush them.

However, Daniel sees that after three and a half years, the court of the Most High G-d convenes before the Ancient of

Days, and the Beast (political leader) is slain by G-d Himself, and his body is destroyed and thrown into the burning fire. The remaining kings have their dominion or authority removed, but an extension of life is given to them for an appointed period of time.

THE WHIRLWIND OF THE LORD

Behold a storm from the Lord has gone forth [with] *fury, yea a settling storm; on the head*[s] *of the wicked it shall rest. The kindling of the Lord's anger shall not return until He has executed it, and until He has fulfilled the plans of His heart. At the end of the days you shall consider it. At that time, says the Lord, I will be the G-d of all the families of Israel, and they shall be My people* (Jeremiah 30:23–25).

Clearly, in the latter days G-d is going to judge and destroy the one who comes and rules over the earth and its inhabitants for three and a half years. He is going to completely destroy him and his kingdom forever.

And the judgment shall be established, and they will remove his dominion to be destroyed and annihilated until the end (Daniel 7:26).

What will replace this most evil kingdom, and who will rule and reign over all the nations and peoples of the earth?

THE LORD'S MESSIAH PRESENTED

I saw in the visions of the night, and behold with the clouds of the heaven, one like a man was coming, and he came up to the Ancient of Days and was brought before Him. And He gave him dominion and glory and a kingdom, and all peoples, nations, and tongues shall serve him; his dominion is an eternal dominion, which will not be removed, and his kingdom is one which will not be destroyed (Daniel 7:13–14).

There can be no doubt as to whom is being described in these prophetic verses. It is the Lord's Messiah.

Daniel sees one like a man coming up to the Ancient of Days, the Father, and the G-d of Israel. He was presented before the G-d of Israel, and to him was given dominion, glory, and a kingdom.

Webster's English dictionary defines the word dominion as follows: "Sovereign or supreme authority; the power of governing and controlling; independent right of possession, use, and control; sovereignty; supremacy."

This is exactly how king Nebuchadnezzar praised and described Daniel's G-d, the G-d of Israel:

Now, I, Nebuchadnezzar, praise and exalt and glorify the King of heaven, Whose works are all true and Whose ways are just and Who can humble those who walk with arrogance (Daniel 4:34).

HIS EVERLASTING KINGDOM

Daniel prophesies that the coming Messiah will establish His kingdom and "all peoples, nations and tongues shall serve Him. His dominion is an eternal dominion which will not be removed; and His kingdom is one which will not be destroyed."

What a promise from the Lord to His people! So let us take heart: though there is going to be a time of great suffering for those who know the Lord, trust the Lord, and walk in His ways and follow His commandments, they will be saved!

YOU CANNOT BE IN THE PRESENCE OF G-D
AND REMAIN THE SAME

One thing is for certain from these verses. You cannot be in the presence of G-d and remain the same. That is absolutely impossible. Daniel was a man who sought to be in the very presence of the Ancient of Days. He was a man with a heart for G-d and for His holy people and nation.

From the day Daniel stood before the throne of the Ancient of Days in Heaven, he was never to be the same. He had seen the Lord and His Messiah and lived. He had experienced G-d, been in His holy presence, and he would never be the same again. Just as we read of Isaiah:

> *In the year that king Uziyyzhu died I saw the Lord sitting upon a Throne, high and lifted up, and his train filled the temple. Serafim stood above him: each one had six wings; with two he covered his face, and with two he covered his feet, and with two he did fly. And one cried to another, and said, Holy, holy, holy, is the Lord of hosts: the whole earth is full of his glory. And the posts of the door moved at the voice of him that cried, and the house was filled with smoke. Then said I, Woe is me! For I am ruined; because I am a man of unclean lips, and I dwell in the midst of a people of unclean lips: for my eyes have seen the King, the Lord of hosts. Then one of the serafim flew to me, having a live coal in his hand, which he had taken with tongs from off the altar: and he laid it upon my mouth, and said, Lo, this has touched thy lips; and thy iniquity is taken away, and thy sin is purged* (Isaiah 6:1–7).[1]

DANIEL: A MAN OF G-D IN AN UNGODLY KINGDOM

Daniel was a man of G-d living in a most ungodly kingdom. There is no question about it: whether you live in Israel, America, or Europe, it is important to understand clearly you are living in an ungodly kingdom. You are no different than Daniel.

While living in an ungodly kingdom that worshiped idols, Daniel was taken up into the throne room of the G-d of Israel and given revelation regarding the future of Israel and the Gentile nations. Once he stood in the presence of G-d, he was never the same. Likewise, if and when you stand in the presence of the Most High G-d, you will never be the same.

The Lord knows you are living in an ungodly kingdom, and He is seeking those who have hearts to be witnesses of the living G-d. He is separating those whom He has chosen to be His witnesses; He is the living G-d of Israel.

As He declared, "I am the G-d of Abraham, Isaac, and Jacob." He never said, "I was the G-d of Abraham, Isaac, and Jacob." He is alive, and likewise they are alive in Heaven with Him, and that is why He declared, "I am," not "I was!"

He is calling you to walk in His ways, not according to the ways of the world and not according to the ways of the coming "evil one" who will rule over the nations for three and a half years (a time, two times, and half a time).

Nothing burdens the heart of G-d more deeply than sin in the hearts and lives of His people. He wants us to see our sin from His perspective, through His eyes, not from our perspective, through human eyes. He is calling us to repent and to deal with our sin and iniquity immediately. He is seeking people who want to enter into His throne room like Daniel, Isaiah, and King David, who cry out to Him, "Blot out our transgressions and cleanse us thoroughly from our iniquities."

Then and only then can we be true witnesses for the living G-d.

Be gracious to me, O G-d, according to Your kindness; according to Your great mercies, erase my transgressions. Wash me thoroughly of my iniquity, and purify me of my sin. For I know my transgressions, and my sin is always before me. Against You alone have I sinned, and I have done what is evil in Your sight, in order that You be justified in Your conduct, and right in Your judgment (Psalm 51:3–6).

He has called us to be a nation of priests, a holy people, to be a light to the nations of the world in order to turn their hearts back to Him. This process must begin with each of us individually so we can first impact our own families, then our nation, and ultimately all the nations of the earth. G-d has called us and all Israel to be His witnesses that He is G-d and there is no savior besides Him.

YOU ARE MY WITNESSES

"You are My witnesses," says the Lord, "and My servant whom I chose, in order that you know and believe Me, and understand that I am He; before Me no G-d was formed and after Me none shall be. I, I am the Lord, and besides Me there is no Savior. I told and I saved, and I made heard and there was no stranger among you, and you are My witnesses," says the Lord, "and I am G-d. Even before the day I am He, and there is no saving from My hand; I do, and who retracts it?" (Isaiah 43:10–13)

This is what our G-d has called us to be—His witnesses! This is what our G-d has called Israel to be—His witnesses!

We are His servants, whom He chose to know and believe that He is G-d, and there was no other G-d formed, and there will be none formed after Him.

He declares, "I, even I, am the Lord, and there is no Savior besides Me!" He tells us, "So you are My witnesses that I am G-d, even from eternity I am He. There is none who can deliver out of My hand; I act and who can reverse it?"

Are you a witness for G-d? Is there evidence in your life that you are one of His witnesses? Is it evident to those around you that you are a godly man or woman living in the midst of a most ungodly nation?

He is calling you to be His witness. Daniel answered the Lord's call. Will you be one who chooses to answer His call?

For the Lord—His eyes run to and fro throughout the entire earth to grant strength with those whose heart is whole toward Him (2 Chronicles 16:9a).

ENDNOTE

1. *The Jerusalem Bible* (Jerusalem: Koren Publishers Jerusalem Ltd, 2000).

Chapter Two

LIFE IN THE MIDST OF THE FIRE

"Did I not cast three men into the fiery furnace, bound?...Behold, I see four free men walking in the midst of the fire, and there is no wound upon them."...Nebuchadnezzar cried out and said, "Blessed be the G-d of Shadrach, Meshach, and Abednego, Who sent His angel and rescued His servants, who trusted Him, deviated from the command of the king, and risked their lives in order not to worship or prostrate themselves to any god except to their G-d" (Daniel 3:24c, 25a, 28).

Most of us do not want to live our lives in the midst of the fire. Shadrach, Meshach, and Abednego did not want to go into the fiery furnace. Daniel did not want to go into the den of lions, and we do not want to have to go into the fire of another war.

However, sometimes the Lord uses real life circumstances to place us in the midst of the fire. Those who know G-d and have for a time lived their lives in the "midst of the fire" will tell you that this is when they were the closest to Him because they knew their lives and very breath were in His hands.

People have asked us, "Why does G-d put us into the fire?" That is a legitimate question, and from personal experience I would say that sometimes He is testing us and sometimes He puts us in the midst of the fire so others can experience G-d through us.

Had Daniel's three friends not been willing to be "cast into the fiery furnace," King Nebuchadnezzar would never have experienced G-d. They were obviously well aware that the king had built an immense statue and that it was his intention that everyone in his kingdom, great and small, be commanded to bow down and worship the statue.

These men exhibited the same character and faith that Daniel had shown them when he refused to eat food sacrificed to idols. Scripture says Daniel "purposed in his heart not to eat the king's food nor drink his wine."

This single verse revealed a great deal about the faith and character of Daniel as a teenager, when he "purposed in his heart" not to eat the king's food and defile himself before G-d. Daniel made up his mind as to what he would do before the circumstances of testing came upon him.

When the time of testing came, there was no decision to be made, because Daniel had already made it. He believed that his G-d would protect him and show him what he was to do to keep from defiling himself by eating food sacrificed to Babylonian idols.

It is interesting to note how Daniel's three friends responded to the king's demand when he summoned them and commanded them to bow down and worship the statue: "O, king, we do not care to answer you about this matter."

> Then Nebuchadnezzar, in wrath and anger, ordered to bring Shadrach, Meshach, and Abednego. Then these men were brought before the king.

> Nebuchadnezzar spoke up and said to them, "Is it [my decree] meaningless, O Shadrach, Meshach, and Abednego, that you do not worship my god and that

you do not prostrate yourselves to the golden image that I have set up?"

Now behold, you are destined, at the time that you hear the whistling horn, the clavichord, the harp, the psaltery, the bagpipes, and all kinds of music, to fall and prostrate yourselves to the image that I made, and if you do not prostrate yourselves, at that time you shall be cast into a burning, fiery furnace, and who is a god who will save you from my hand?

Shadrach, Meshach, and Abednego answered and said to the king, "Nebuchadnezzar, we do not care to answer you about this matter. Behold there is our G-d whom we worship; He can save us. From the burning, fiery furnace and from your hands, O king, He will save [us]. And if not, let it be known to you, O king, that we will not worship your god, neither will we prostrate ourselves to the golden image that you have set up" (Daniel 3:13–18).

Immediately, the king commanded the furnace to be heated seven times hotter than normal. Then, he ordered Daniel's three friends to be bound hand and foot and cast into the midst of the fiery furnace.

After casting them into the midst of the fiery furnace the king suddenly beheld a fourth man in the midst of the fire, walking around with the three young men with their bonds loosed from their hands and feet. King Nebuchadnezzar knew what had transpired before him—the living G-d of Israel had saved the young men and set them free because of their faith in Him.

Can you imagine the awe and astonishment that must have gripped the king and those who had accused Daniel's friends? Can you imagine the fear this must have put into their hearts?

ATTITUDE ADJUSTMENT

Then King Nebuchadnezzar was bewildered and stood up in haste. He shouted and said to his leaders, "Did I not cast three men into the fiery furnace, bound?" They answered and said to the king, "The king is true."

He called out and said, "Behold, I see four free men walking in the midst of the fire, and there is no wound upon them, and the form of the fourth one is like [that of] an angel."

Then Nebuchadnezzar approached the gate of the burning, fiery furnace. He shouted and said, "Shadrach, Meshach, and Abednego, the servants of the Most High G-d! Step out and come!" Then Shadrach, Meshach, and Abednego came out of the midst of the fire (Daniel 3:24–26).

Notice how the king now addresses Daniel's three friends, when he calls them to come out of the fire, "Step out and come, you servants of the Most High G-d."

Suddenly, there was fear, reverence, and profound respect in the king's voice. He had had an experience with the living G-d of Israel and had suffered a profound attitude adjustment.

What did the king and his high officials see in the midst of the fiery furnace? Nebuchadnezzar had cried out, "Behold, I see four free men walking in the midst of the fire, and there is no wound upon them, and the form of the fourth one is like [that of] an angel."

Notice what the King declared once they came out:

Nebuchadnezzar cried out and said, "Blessed be the G-d of Shadrach, Meshach, and Abednego, Who sent His angel and rescued His servants, who trusted Him, deviated from the command of the king, and risked their lives in order not to worship or prostrate themselves to any god except to their G-d. Now an order is issued by me that any people, nation, or tongue that will speak amiss about the G-d of Shadrach, Meshach, and Abednego shall be torn limb from limb and his house shall be made a dungheap because there is no other god who can save in this manner." Then the king made

Shadrach, Meshach, and Abednego prosper in the capital city of Babylon (Daniel 3:28–30).

The king said, "There is no other G-d who is able to deliver in this way."

What if Daniel's friends had chosen to bow down and worship the king's idol? King Nebuchadnezzar and his officials would never have experienced the saving power of the living G-d of Israel.

They were witnesses to the faith that Daniel's three friends had boldly professed in their G-d, no matter the consequences. The officials all knew they were standing in the presence of three men who did not fear man but instead feared and revered their G-d.

Sometimes we have to be willing to walk in the midst of the fire so those around us will experience the saving power of the living G-d of Israel. Sometimes the Lord causes some of us to walk in the midst of the fire so even people who profess to believe in G-d but have never really experienced Him will come to know Him, as the living G-d.

There are many people today who know *about* G-d but have never *experienced* G-d. There is a great deal of difference between knowing about someone and actually knowing them personally. The same is true with the Lord.

When you are about to be thrown into the midst of the fire, it is not what you say that reveals what you believe about G-d—it's what you are willing to do! You cannot know the Lord intimately unless you have personally experienced Him in real-life circumstances. I have found that it is not really important what people say about their faith in G-d, but rather it is what they do when He places them in the midst of the fiery furnace that truly reveals what they believe about G-d.

People can speak about matters of faith and trust in the Lord, they can quote verses from the Tanach and act piously, they can pray three times a day, but it is only when they are smitten, in the midst of the fire, with their actions open to the scrutiny of others, that one can tell what they really believe about the living G-d.

There are no shortcuts with G-d. There is nowhere to hide in the midst of the fire. There is no room to maneuver or to compromise. There is only you and the Lord and the fire! Either you trust and believe in Him or you don't. Nothing in the midst of the fire is hidden from G-d!

We have written a great deal about horrendous events that are soon to come upon all the inhabitants of the earth. Only the living G-d of Israel can forgive your sins, save you, redeem you, and protect and provide for you. He is the only One who can be your shield and defense.

This book has been written using the examples of Daniel and his three friends to encourage you and to expand your faith and trust in G-d. It has been written so you will not be deceived when the time of "Jacob's trouble" arrives. You will instead be like Daniel and his three friends. You will be witnesses that your G-d is the one and only true and living G-d, the Holy One of Israel. Because of this you will be able to recognize the coming supposed "friend of the Jews," who, with smooth words and ruthless cunning, will seek to deceive all Israel.

Because you know and trust your G-d, like Daniel, you can purpose in your heart what you will do if you are commanded to bow down and worship an image of this evil king who proclaims himself a god. You will be able to stand as a witness because you "purposed in your heart beforehand what you would do."

So do not fear when the Lord puts you in the midst of the fire; rather, exercise your faith. Pray expectantly, walk expectantly, and believe He is with you, and then others will see and know that our Lord lives and that He is able to deliver from the fiery furnace—because He is the living G-d, the Holy One of Israel.

Only when you have been in the midst of the fire can you purpose to walk out, empowered by the Holy Spirit of G-d, to be a witness so strong that no one can deny that your G-d is the One true living G-d, who rules and reigns amidst no other in heaven or on earth!

> *"Here is the G-d of my salvation, I shall trust and not fear; for the strength and praise of the Eternal the Lord was my salvation." And you shall draw water with joy from the fountains of the salvation. And you shall say on that day, "Thank the Lord, call in His Name, publicize His deeds among the peoples; keep it in remembrance, for His Name is exalted. Sing to the Lord for He has performed mighty deeds; this is known throughout the land. Shout and praise, O dwellers of Zion, for great in your midst is the Holy One of Israel"* (Isaiah 12:2–6).

Chapter Three

BIRTHRIGHT

The burden of the word of the Lord to Israel in the hand of Malachi. I loved you, said the Lord, and you said, "How have You loved us?" Was not Esau a brother to Jacob? says the Lord. And I loved Jacob. And I hated Esau, and I made his mountains desolate and his heritage into [a habitat for] *the jackals of the desert* (Malachi 1:1–3).

In these prophetic verses we see that the Lord loved Jacob, whose name He later changed to Israel. But the Tanach goes on to say, "I hated Esau, and I made his mountains desolate and his heritage into [a habitat for] the jackals of the desert."

Why did the Lord love Jacob and hate his brother, Esau? The reason is that Esau despised his birthright. He was the son of Isaac and the grandson of Abraham, whom the G-d of Israel had promised to bless beyond measure.

The Lord G-d of Israel had said to Abraham:

That I will surely bless you, and I will greatly multiply your seed as the stars of the heavens and as the sand that is on the seashore, and your descendants will inherit the cities of their enemies. And through your children shall be blessed all the nations of the world, because you hearkened to My voice (Genesis 22:17–18).

Esau was the first-born son of Isaac and heir to G-d's promised blessings to his grandfather Abraham. No other man ever received such promises from G-d like those given to Abraham, and according to Jewish law they were to be passed down to Esau from Isaac. The Lord G-d of Israel promised Abraham that "in your seed all the nations of the earth shall be blessed!"

The great blessing that all the nations of the earth were to receive through Abraham's lineage was the Messiah. From Abraham the promise of this blessing would be passed to Isaac, and then on to Esau. However, the Tanach reveals that Esau despised his birthright. Consequently, the blessing promised to Abraham could never be passed down through his lineage to Esau, so the Lord instead transferred the blessing to Jacob. The lineage of Jacob is traced to Jesse, the father of King David, and from the Tanach we know that the Messiah will come from the lineage of King David.

ESAU SELLS HIS BIRTHRIGHT FOR A POT OF STEW

Now Jacob cooked a pottage, and Esau came from the field, and he was faint. And Esau said to Jacob, "Pour into [me] *some of this red, red* [pottage], *for I am faint"; he was therefore named Edom. And Jacob said, "Sell me as of this day your birthright." Esau replied, "Behold, I am going to die; so why do I need this birthright?" And Jacob said, "Swear to me as of this day"; so he swore to him, and he sold his birthright to Jacob. And Jacob gave Esau bread and a pottage of lentils, and he ate and drank and arose and left, and Esau despised the birthright* (Genesis 25:29–34).

Esau placed more value on a pot of lentil stew than he did on his birthright. Even though his father favored him as the firstborn, G-d had heard Esau's words, seen his actions, and above all, knew his heart.

Esau did not understand that he was created by G-d for an eternal purpose—to preserve the lineage that would someday bring forth the Messiah. He did not understand that everything G-d does has an eternal purpose. When G-d gave His promises to Abraham, it was done with a divine vision of eternal blessings for all humankind. G-d's perspective is different from human perspective. His plans transcend our concept of time, and His perspective extends beyond the here and now. People are often more concerned with watching the latest movie and other self-centered acts than they are in seeking an understanding of G-d's eternal plan for their lives. While G-d certainly doesn't ask us to go hungry, Esau's tragic mistake was his prideful disdain of his rightful place in G-d's eternal plan. Esau didn't believe or care that G-d would do such a marvelous thing through him, choosing instead to satisfy the growling of an empty stomach, a stomach that, once filled, would soon become empty once again.

How many of us run the risk of missing the eternal blessing that G-d intends for us simply because we don't believe that we are worthy to be chosen for His intended purpose, shortcomings and all? G-d has a plan for all of us for good, not for evil, and it does not depend upon our worthiness. However, it does depend upon whether or not we give Him our whole hearts. He is able to do the rest.

> *For I know the thoughts that I think about you, says the Lord, thoughts of peace and not of evil, to give you a future and a hope. And you shall call Me and go and pray to Me, and I will hearken to you. And you will seek Me and find [Me] for you will seek Me with all your heart. And I will be found by you, says the Lord, and I will return your captivity and gather you from all the nations and from all the places where I have driven you, says the Lord, and I will return you to the place whence I exiled you* (Jeremiah 29:11–14).

The Tanach says Esau's name was later called Edom, and from that point forward his name became synonymous with the location of Edom for all eternity. Much of the conflict today in the Middle East has to do with the descendants of Esau seeking to reclaim a birthright that is no longer theirs by killing their brother's children, the Jewish people, and stealing the inheritance in the land G-d promised as an everlasting possession.

PROPHECY AGAINST MOUNT SEIR AND EDOM

Then the word of the Lord came to me, saying: "Son of man, direct your face toward Mount Seir and prophesy over it. And you shall say to it: So said the Lord G-d: Behold I am against you, O Mount Seir, and I shall stretch forth My hand upon you and make you desolate and waste. I shall lay your cities waste, and you will be desolate, and you will know that I am the Lord" (Ezekiel 35:1–4).

Mount Seir is located in Edom, and throughout the Tanach Mount Seir and Edom are linked together.

The G-d of Israel reveals His feelings toward Mount Seir and Edom in the verses above when He declares, "I shall stretch forth My hand upon you and make you desolate and waste. I shall lay your cities waste, and you will be desolate."

What a prophetic word of disaster and destruction! Why has the Lord decreed complete destruction on Mount Seir and Edom?

The first reason is found in the last verse of the prophecy: "And you will know that I am the Lord." Edom shall come to know that the G-d of Israel is G-d and not Allah!

The second reason is this:

Because you had everlasting hatred, and you hurled the children of Israel by the sword, on the day of their misfortune at the time of the end of their iniquity. Therefore, as I live, says the Lord G-d, for I shall make you into blood, and blood will pursue you; for surely you hated blood, and blood will pursue you (Ezekiel 35:5–6).

In these verses we see Edom had "everlasting hatred" against the sons of Israel, a hatred that runs through all of human history. Edom's initial sin against Israel occurred when they refused Israel passage through their territory during the Exodus from Egypt in the days of Moses.

During the 1930s and 1940s the Jewish people faced their worst crisis since the destruction of the Temple by the Romans, as Adolph Hitler sought to completely exterminate all Jews living in Europe. For a short period of time, pressure from the Zionist movement opened the doors to the Promised Land, allowing some of the Jews to escape from Europe. However, the British slammed the door shut at the insistence of Edom (the Arab nations with the spirit of Edom), thereby condemning millions of Jews to death in Hitler's extermination camps.

Just as G-d's word said, "They hurled the sons of Israel by the sword, on the day of their misfortune." The Arab riots, political pressure and threats caused the British to finally close the door to the Jews who sought asylum in Israel prior to WWII.

This theme is so strong in the mind of G-d that He repeats it again in the book of Obadiah. The ire of the Lord is aroused against Edom and Esau for their sins against Israel.

FOR YOUR OUTRAGE AGAINST YOUR BROTHER JACOB

Because of the violence of your brother Jacob, shame shall cover you, and you shall be cut off forever. On that day you stood from afar, on the day strangers captured his possessions, and foreigners came into his cities, and on Jerusalem they cast lots; you, too, are like one of them. And you should not have looked on the day of your brother on the day of his being delivered, and you should not have rejoiced about the children of Judah on the day of their destruction, and you should not have spoken proudly on the day of distress.

You should not have come into the gate of My people on the day of their misfortune; you too should not have looked at their affliction on the day of their misfortune, and you should not have stretched out [your hand] upon their possessions on the day of their misfortune. And you should not have stood by the gap to cut off their fugitives, neither should you have delivered their survivors on the day of distress. For the day of the Lord over all the nations is close; as you have done shall be done to you; your recompense shall be returned upon your head (Obadiah 1:10–15).

The Lord takes an eternal view of Edom's crimes against Israel. G-d takes issue with the way the Arab-Muslim nations have historically exhibited hatred and animosity towards the Jewish people. From G-d's eternal perspective His covenant with Abraham has never been broken because from the beginning it was an unconditional covenant that depended not upon Israel's faithfulness but rather on the immutable word and promises of G-d.

SATAN SEEKS TO ROB A NATION AND A PEOPLE OF THEIR BIRTHRIGHT

Israel's promise of the land has never ceased to exist. The Palestinians, supported by the E.U., America, Russia, the Arab nations, and the UN today, continue to make illegitimate claim to the land promised by G-d to the descendants of Abraham, Isaac and Jacob (not Esau).

The Palestinians are seeking to take the land of Israel, the G-d-promised birthright of the Jewish people. The nations are seeking to force Israel to give over her birthright and inheritance in Judea, Samaria, and east Jerusalem to the Palestinians, who still operate in the spirit of Esau and Edom.

The Muslim nations' eternal hatred for Israel has a dual purpose. They are not just seeking to force Israel to give up the land but are also conspiring together in seeking the complete and total destruction of the Jewish people.

The president of Iran has repeatedly declared that the solution to the problems in the Middle East is the destruction of the nation of Israel, a destruction so complete that the name of Israel will be remembered no more.

The nations of the world brought forth the Oslo Peace Process, which was founded on one basic principal—the concept of trading Israel's land for peace. The nations said to Israel, *Just forsake your birthright and give it over to those who worship Allah, and you will have peace.*

The nations today are continually pressuring, threatening, and making war against Israel, using every means at their disposal to force Israel to turn away from G-d's covenant and forsake her birthright.

WHAT THE NATIONS DEMAND OF ISRAEL— FORSAKE YOUR G-D!

First, forsake your G-d.

Second, forsake His covenant promises with you.

Third, forsake and give over your birthright in the land He promised you as an everlasting possession.

Fourth, forsake and surrender your control over G-d's holy city, Jerusalem, and give control of His holy mountain to those who worship Allah.

These are all covenant issues, comprising the very heart of the matter that revolves around the question of who G-d really is—the covenant-keeping G-d of Abraham, or the god of Islam, Allah?

G-d's covenant with Israel is eternal and everlasting. However the evil one, the serpent of old, has, since the creation, opposed the plans and purposes of G-d. Today he is using his power to cause the nations of the earth to rise up and force Israel to surrender her birthright and give it over to those who serve Allah—all in the name of a false peace.

In every generation the evil one has raised up nations and peoples to persecute, kill, harass, and expel the Jewish people.

The evil one has not changed—he has been the implacable enemy of G-d and G-d's people from the beginning of time.

As in the time of Daniel, G-d has allowed the Prince of Persia to once again rise up, empowered by the evil one, in order to complete the destruction of Israel and the Jewish people. The president of Iran and his Arab-Muslim allies have made a covenant together against the G-d of Israel and the Jewish people, that the name of Israel will be remembered no more.

Today another part of the evil one's strategy is to cause the Jewish people to commit the sin of Esau by despising their birthright and exchanging the promise of eternal blessing for the false hope of a temporal "false peace" brought about by politicians and diplomats. The plans of the evil one have never changed, and Israel's history of apostasy and her tendency towards forgetfulness of G-d's unconditional promises play directly into the hand of him who would destroy her.

CONSTANT PRESSURE AND WAR

Since her birth as a nation in 1948, Israel has experienced more wars, more terror, more violence, more political pressure, and more threats than any other nation on earth. Today the people of Israel have grown weary of war, terror, and violence.

The Arab-Muslim nations launched wars against Israel in 1948, 1956, 1967, and 1973. In the 1980s Israel has suffered war in Lebanon, two Palestinian intifadas, the rise of Hamas, and the missile attacks of 2005 and 2006, and the Hezbollah war in Lebanon in July and August of 2006. It is a fact that no nation on earth has experienced what Israel has been forced to endure at the hands of her Muslim neighbors.

Today, as in the past, whenever Israel is attacked and seeks to defend herself, the E.U., the UN, and most of the nations of the world take the side of Islam. The news media condemn Israel daily for defending herself and regularly repeat the charge that Israel is using "excessive force" and is guilty of "war crimes."

Incredibly, this same perspective holds true concerning the latest war in Lebanon, during which, Hezbollah crossed over Israel's international border, attacked and killed Israeli soldiers, kidnapped more Israeli soldiers, and then proceeded to launch over 4,000 rockets and missiles into Israeli cities, many from Lebanon's civilian population centers. But according to the world's news media, Israel is the unjustified aggressor in seeking to defend herself.

WOE TO THOSE WHO CALL EVIL GOOD AND GOOD EVIL!

We are living in an evil time, when the world calls that which is evil good and that which is good evil. Nowhere is this fact more evident than in most of the world's media. The power of television to depict images of suffering around the world can often be used to mold public opinion against the truth. Truth is flung to the ground, and deception is everywhere. The evil of murdering Israeli soldiers, kidnapping others, and launching thousands of rockets into Israeli cities goes largely unchallenged by the world's media.

Yet when Israel defends herself and is forced to go into civilian population centers to destroy missiles being launched from their midst, it stands guilty of war crimes! What about the men who deliberately placed their launching sites and headquarters in the very midst of their own citizens? Who are the real murderers here? Who are really guilty of "war crimes"? Those who launched the missiles? Those who knowingly placed them in the midst of their civilian population? No, it is Israel, declares the world's media.

> *Woe to those who say of the evil that it is good and of the good that it is evil; who present darkness as light and light as darkness, who present bitter as sweet and sweet as bitter.* (Isaiah 5:20).

The terrible plight of the Lebanese civilian population is again and again broadcast around the world, showcasing dozens of wounded or dead children. The E.U. meets and decides to contribute millions of euros to Lebanon's people for reconstruction. Yet for most of the war, over one million Israelis were forced to live in bomb shelters or flee for their lives as the rockets rained down on them and their cities.

Where are the millions of euros needed to rebuild the shattered lives, homes and businesses of thousands of Israelis? Why was there no help offered by the E.U. to the hundreds of thousands of Israelis whose lives have been permanently altered by the fear of perpetual violence originating from the Lebanese border? To date not a single euro has been offered, doubtless because of Israel's "disproportionate response" to the rain of 4,000 rockets that caused untold terror and wreaked havoc amidst her northern cities.

Why is there no serious condemnation of Hezbollah coming from the world's news media, from the UN, or from the E.U.?

BECAUSE YOU HAD EVERLASTING HATRED TOWARD THE SONS OF ISRAEL!

There is no help for Israel, and there is no serious condemnation of Hezbollah because the world today calls that which is good evil and that which is evil good. There is little empathy or understanding expressed for the Jewish people because the E.U., the media, Russia, and the UN all appear to have received a portion of that spirit of Esau and Edom which fills the Muslim nations. Just as G-d's word says: "Because you had everlasting hatred...." (Ezekiel 35:5).

The spirit of Esau is often reflected in the attitudes and responses of the nations and the international news media, betraying a hardening of heart towards G-d's chosen people. The Tanach seems to indicate that this manifestation of enmity will continue to grow as we move closer to the advent of the Fourth Kingdom.

ISRAEL—GO IN AND POSSESS THE LAND I PROMISED YOU

Today modern Israel is exactly like the generation that lived in the days of Moses, Joshua, and Caleb. G-d commanded that generation to go in and possess the land He promised them according to His everlasting covenant.

G-d commanded Moses to send 12 men to spy out the land, with one man being selected from each of Israel's 12 tribes. They were told to bring back a report to Moses and the people about the land of Canaan and its inhabitants.

When the men returned, they brought back with them some of the beautiful fruit of the land to show the people. However, their report was a bad report, and it put fear, not faith, into the hearts of the people. They said,

> *"We are unable to go up against the people, for they are stronger than we. They spread an [evil] report about the land which they had scouted, telling the children of Israel, The land we passed through to explore is a land that consumes its inhabitants, and all the people we saw in it are men of stature. There we saw the giants, the sons of Anak, descended from the giants. In our eyes, we seemed like grasshoppers, and so we were in their eyes"* (Numbers 13:31–33).

THERE ARE GIANTS IN THE LAND!

They began their report declaring, "We are unable to go up against the people, for they are stronger than we." Their words revealed what was in their hearts. They had no faith or trust in the promises made to them by the living G-d of Israel when He brought them out of Egypt, and they therefore cried out in fear saying, "we seemed like grasshoppers, and so we were in their eyes."

THE PROMISES OF G-D

Will you say to yourself, "These nations are more numerous than I; how will I be able to drive them out"? You shall not fear them. You shall surely remember what the Lord, your G-d, did to Pharaoh and to all of Egypt: the great trials that your eyes saw, the signs, the wonders, the mighty hand, and the outstretched arm with which the Lord, your G-d, brought you out. So will the Lord, Your G-d, do to all the peoples you fear. And also the tzir'ah, the Lord, your G-d, will incite against them, until the survivors and those who hide from you perish. You shall not be terrified of them, for the Lord, your G-d, Who is in your midst, is a great and awesome G-d. And the Lord, your G-d, will drive out those nations from before you, little by little. You will not be able to destroy them quickly, lest the beasts of the field outnumber you. But the Lord, your G-d, will deliver them to you, and He will confound them with great confusion, until they are destroyed. And He will deliver their kings into your hand, and you will destroy their name from beneath the heavens; no man will be able to stand up before you, until you have destroyed them (Deuteronomy 7:17–24).

During the days of Moses the Lord made awesome promises to the children of Israel when He commanded them to go in and possess the land.

- You shall not fear them.

- Remember what I did to Pharaoh and all of Egypt.

- Remember the great trials that your eyes saw, the signs, wonders, the mighty hand, and the outstretched arm with which the Lord brought you out.

- Understand that so will I do to all the peoples you fear.

- Understand the tzir'ah, which the Lord, your G-d, will incite against them.

- You shall not be terrified of them, for the Lord, our G-d, who is in your midst, is a great and awesome G-d.

- The Lord your G-d will drive out those nations before you.

- The Lord your G-d will deliver them to you and confound them with great confusion until they are destroyed.

- He will deliver their kings into your hand.

- No man will be able to stand up before you until you have destroyed them.

Yet in spite of all G-d's promises to Israel, they preferred to focus on the great size and height of the people. The spies had interpreted what their eyes had seen from a human perspective, rather than steeling their hearts and obediently looking to their G-d and His unfailing promises.

The people feared man more than they feared G-d! They looked to their own wisdom, their own strength, and their own flesh, rather than to the power, wisdom, promises, and strength of their G-d.

A MAN WITH ANOTHER SPIRIT

But as for My servant Caleb, since he was possessed by another spirit, and he followed Me, I will bring him to the land to which he came, and his descendants will drive it[s inhabitants] *out....You shall* [not] *come into the Land concerning which I raised My hand that you would settle in it, except Caleb the son of Jephunneh and Joshua the son of Nun. As for your infants, of whom you said that they will be as spoils, I will bring them* [there], *and they will come to know the Land which You despised. But as for you, your corpses shall fall in this desert* (Numbers 14:24,30–32).

There were two men out of the 12 whom the Lord declared had another spirit and had followed Him. These two men were Caleb and Joshua. These two men believed the promises of G-d and stood to encourage the people in the exercise of their faith.

Caleb silenced the people to [hear about] *Moses, and he said, "We can surely go up and take possession of it, for we can indeed overcome it."*

Joshua the son of Nun and Caleb the son of Jephunneh, who were among those who had scouted the land, tore their clothes. They spoke to the entire congregation of the children of Israel, saying, "The land we passed through to scout is an exceedingly good land. If the Lord desires us, He will bring us to this land and give it to us, a land flowing with milk and honey. But you shall not rebel against the Lord, and you will not fear the people of that land for they are [as] our bread. Their protection is removed from them, and the Lord is with us; do not be fear them." The entire congregation threatened to pelt them with stones, but the glory of the Lord appeared in the Tent of Meeting to all the children of Israel (Numbers 13:30; 14:6–10).

Joshua, and Caleb, were men who possessed another spirit, and their words to the people revealed what they believed about their G-d. During a time of testing, all that really matters is a willingness to simply take G-d at His word.

Caleb and Joshua encouraged action as they exercised their faith, even though all the congregation of Israel sought to stone them. Look carefully at what they said to the people:

- We should by all means go up and take possession of the land, for we will surely overcome it.

- If the Lord is pleased with us, then He will bring us into this land and give it to us.

- Do not rebel against the Lord.

- Do not fear the people of the land, for they are our prey.

- Their protection has been removed from them.

- The Lord is with us; do not fear them.

These men did not look at the circumstances but rather to their G-d. Joshua and Caleb did not fear man—they feared the living G-d of Israel.

These men were among the appointed leaders of Israel, yet the people refused to listen to them, thereby rebelling against the command of G-d and, because of their unbelief, causing that entire generation of the faithless to die in the desert, never to enter the land G-d promised to them.

MODERN ISRAEL: A NATION WHOSE LEADERS AND PEOPLE DO NOT FEAR THE LIVING G-D OF ISRAEL

Modern Israel in the twenty-first century is a great deal like the congregation of Israel that lived in the days of Moses, Joshua, and Caleb. Israel's leaders do not believe in the G-d of Israel, nor do they believe in His covenant promises regarding the land. In modern Israel today there is absolutely no fear of the living G-d because they foolishly refuse to believe that He is who He says He is and believe He is able to fulfill His promises.

Because there is no fear of the living G-d, apostasy and un-belief have infected the leaders and people of Israel, rendering them blind and unable to understand their circumstances in light of the covenant and therefore are unwilling to "hold fast and push through" in order that they may inherit and possess the birthright.

FALSE INTEGRITY MEANS A FALSE PEACE

In the recent war in Lebanon (July–August 2006), the strat-egy of Israel's leaders conspicuously failed to include the blow-ing of the shofar, the calling for a fast, and the seeking of G-d's wisdom and strategy for the war. Based upon the outcome of the war and the manner in which it was waged, it is doubtful that there was ever a real strategy for complete and total victory.

In G-d's eyes there is no substitute for victory. Israel's lead-ers are not like Joshua or Caleb. Their hearts are exactly like the faithless people of Israel in the time of Moses. They fear man, not G-d. They fear the wrath of America and the nations, not G-d's wrath. They trust in the United Nations to protect them rather than the G-d of Israel.

There were thousands of Israelis, young and old, who were willing to fight and die to win the war in Lebanon in order to completely shatter the power of Hezbollah so it could not rise again. However, the root of the problem from a human per-spective did not reside in Lebanon with Hezbollah, but rather in Damascus and Tehran. Unfortunately, neither Jerusalem nor Washington was ready to confront the root issue, so G-d gave victory into the hands of Israel's enemies.

Because Israel's leaders placed their trust in men and diplomacy and continue to do so, they were, and still are, willing to settle for a false peace that will only set the stage for the next war, which will almost certainly be bigger and more terrible. In the future, there will be unrelenting pressure from the nations for Israel to "show good faith" by ceding her birthright in Judea, Samaria, and east Jerusalem. Because of Israel's unbelief and unwillingness to trust in her G-d and follow His commandments, they will run the risk of forsaking their birthright.

Unless our leaders repent and call the people to turn back to the living G-d, they will continue to lead Israel down a path of war, terror, and destruction. Israel cannot forsake her G-d and expect any other result. Israel's entire history as a people and nation is a living testimony to this unshakable truth.

NO FEAR OF THEIR G-D—NO FEAR OF SIN

Loss of the fear of their G-d has caused Israelis to lose their fear of sin. Once the fear of sin is lost, there ceases to be a reference point by which actions and behaviors can be judged and interpreted. This makes it inevitable for the people to compromise their faith and look to diplomats and politicians for their salvation, rather than to their G-d. Do you think for one minute that King David would have ever given up Gaza, Judea, and Samaria to the Philistines, much less half of Jerusalem?

Modern-day Israelis willfully emulate the nations who worship gods of gold, silver, and oil. Sin has clouded the lenses of our eyes, and iniquity has hardened the fibers of our hearts so that we cannot embrace G-d's covenant promises regarding the land and our inheritance. As we and our leaders turn more and more to follow the ways of the world, we lose the knowledge of our G-d and His commandments, and the blessings that come from following His ways.

When we the people and our leaders lose the knowledge of G-d and His commandments, we become separated from our covenant connection with the land G-d promised us as an everlasting possession. Once this connection is broken, we become willing to exchange our covenant-promised land for a false peace.

HOPE IS NOURISHED BY FAITH AND TRUST IN G-D

Hope is nourished by faith, and after years of war, faithless Israelis have lost hope. Our sin of unbelief, combined with the weariness resulting from endless wars, terror, and violence, along with unrelenting pressure from the nations, has set the stage for the unthinkable—willful abandonment of territory supernaturally restored to Jewish control after almost two thousand years of exile and dispersion so that G-d's prophetic plan and purpose might be fulfilled—the complete reconciliation and restoration of the faithful remnant of the house of Israel.

As faith refreshes hope, so may a new burst of faith strengthen us in our weariness. Esau's yielding to his hunger resulted in the abandonment of his birthright. Today in Israel, our weariness is leavened by our faithlessness, and, like Esau, we contemplate the abandonment of our national birthright.

You see, the eye of faith perceives unseen reality and believes it will come to pass. Faith is the power to see and understand those things that are not perceived by worldly senses.

The great men of G-d like Abraham, Moses, Joshua, Caleb, David, Elijah, Isaiah, Jeremiah, Ezekiel, and Daniel all believed that a life of faith and trust was sure to be rewarded by the blessing of G-d. When trials came, they all persevered rather than giving up. David's secret was that he paid no attention to his own weaknesses and inabilities. His eye of faith was solely on his G-d and deliverer.

Just as David cried out to the Lord G-d to create a clean heart and renew a steadfast spirit within him, Israel too needs to cry out for spiritual renewal. If they will do this with sincere hearts, the G-d of Israel will pour out His Spirit upon His people. *Only then, when there is a cleansing and renewing of our hearts, will Israel claim the power and authority to fully possess her birthright.* Spiritual renewal will bring forth a supernatural faith that will glorify G-d himself among the nations, in accordance with Israel's divine calling. G-d has promised to preserve and bring forth a remnant that believes His promises and is willing to act accordingly no matter what the circumstances or the consequences. Are you willing to be called as part of G-d's faithful remnant? Have you learned to hear His voice so that you might respond and be saved?

"Not by military force and not by physical strength, but by My spirit," says the Lord of Hosts (Zechariah 4:6).

TODAY, ISRAEL'S FAITH IS BEING TESTED

Without exercise and stretching, muscles will not grow and develop. Faith is like a muscle. It must be exercised repeatedly, to its limits and beyond, if it is to expand and develop.

Trials, obstacles, challenges, difficulties, and sometimes defeat are the food for growing our faith. Israel may fail the test of faith for a season, but the G-d of Israel will never fail, nor will His covenant promises fail to come to pass for His nation and His people.

MOSES PLEADS FOR THE PEOPLE

The Lord said to Moses, "How long will this people provoke Me? How much longer will they not believe in Me after all the signs I have performed in their midst? I will strike them with a plague and annihilate them; then I will make you into a nation, greater and stronger than they."

Moses said to the Lord, "But the Egyptians will hear that You have brought this nation out from its midst with great power. They will say about the inhabitants of this land, who have heard that You, O Lord, are in the midst of this people; that You, the Lord, appear to them eye to eye and that Your cloud rests over them. And You go before them with a pillar of cloud by day and with a pillar of cloud by night, and if You kill this nation like one man, the nations who have heard of Your reputation will say as follows:

'Since the Lord lacked the ability to bring this nation to the Land which He swore to them, He slaughtered them in the desert.' Now, please, let the strength of the Lord be increased, as You spoke, saying.

'The Lord is slow to anger and abundantly kind, forgiving iniquity and transgression, Who cleanses [some] *and does not cleanse* [others]*, Who visits the iniquities of parents on children, even to the third and fourth generations.'*

"Please forgive the iniquity of this nation in accordance with your abounding kindness, as You have borne this people from Egypt until now" (Numbers 14:11–19).

Today, people of faith need to stand in the gap before the Lord on behalf of our people, just as Moses did. We need to pray that the Lord G-d of Israel will pardon the iniquity of our people according to the greatness of His loving kindness.

Pray that He will show us mercy. Pray the Lord will pour out His Spirit of grace and supplication on the house of Judah and Israel to heal us, protect us, and save us from our enemies and ourselves.

IF MY PEOPLE WILL HUMBLE THEMSELVES AND PRAY

And My people, upon whom My name is called, humble themselves and pray and seek My presence and repent of their evil ways, I shall hear from heaven and forgive their sin and heal their land. Now, My eyes will be open and My ears attentive to the prayer of this place (2 Chronicles 7:14–15).

Will you be one who will humble yourself before the Lord G-d of Israel and pray and seek His face? Will you be one who will turn from your wicked ways and repent before the living G-d? Only then will He hear from Heaven, forgive our sins, pour out His Spirit of grace and supplication on the house of Israel and the house of Judah, heal our land, and save our people from our enemies.

The Lord's eyes are open, and His ears are attentive to see if you and I will be as Moses, who stood in the gap before the Lord for our people in the desert. He kept the Lord from destroying the entire nation from the earth. Are you one of G-d's remnant, who will be as Daniel was before G-d on behalf of His people?

And I prayed to the Lord my G-d, and I confessed, and I said, "Please, O Lord, O great and awesome G-d, Who keeps the covenant and the loving-kindness to those who love Him and keep His commandments. We have sinned and have dealt iniquitously; we have dealt wickedly and have rebelled, turning away from Your commandments and from Your ordinances....

"To You, O Lord, is the righteousness, and to us is the shamefacedness as of this day, to the people of Judah, to the inhabitants of Jerusalem, and to all Israel both near and far, in all the lands to which you have driven them for the treachery that they have perpetrated toward You....

"O Lord, hear; O Lord, forgive; O Lord, hearken and do, do not delay; for Your sake, my G-d, for Your Name is called upon Your city and upon Your people."

Now I was still speaking and praying and confessing my sin and the sin of my people Israel and casting my supplication before the Lord my G-d about the mount of the Sanctuary of my G-d. While I was still speaking in prayer, the man Gabriel, whom I saw in the vision at first, approached me in swift flight about the time of the evening offering. And he enabled me to understand, and he spoke with me, and he said, "Daniel, now I have come forth to make you skillful in understanding" (Daniel 9:4–5,7,19–22).

If we become as Solomon or Daniel, humbly prostrating ourselves before the G-d of Abraham, Isaac, and Jacob, the living G-d, the Holy One of Israel, surely He will give us understanding of the things to take place in the days to come.

Chapter Four

FALSE PEACE

For both prophet and priest are false; even in My house
have I found their evil, says the Lord (Jeremiah 23:11).

Since the so-called Oslo Peace Process began in the early 1990s, followed by the American-sponsored Road Map for Peace, we have witnessed an endless procession of Israeli leaders who declare that by retreating and giving over our inheritance to the worshipers of Allah, Israel will gain permanent peace with security. For more than thirteen years these leaders, in conjunction with the media, have continually repeated the mantra of giving up land for peace. Yet each time Israel has given away a portion of its inheritance, the result has been sadly predictable. Israel's leaders and the media all said "Peace, peace," yet what came forth was not peace, but war, terror, suicide bombers, and missiles.

The Quartet of Nations (the United States, Russia, the European Union, and the United Nations), along with Israel's political leaders and the media, have continually promoted a policy of retreat and surrender, reaffirming the idea that the Israeli people have no choice but to give over their eternal inheritance in the land G-d promised them to the god of Islam. Only then will they have peace and security.

Again, I ask the question: "What has been the result of Oslo and the Road Map?" Have they produced peace? In reality, everyone living in Israel today knows they have produced just the opposite—a never-ending series of attacks and skirmishes that continue to weigh heavily upon the hearts and minds of all Israelis. The true spawn and spin of the diplomats is not peace but deception, terror, and death.

The Nations' Road Map to Peace has birthed the rise to power of Hamas in Gaza. Since Israel's unilateral withdrawal, Hamas has deliberately caused hundreds of missiles to rain down on the Israeli cities surrounding Gaza.

Israel's unilateral withdrawal from Lebanon under the formula of retreat and surrender has also given rise to Hezbollah in Lebanon, armed with thousands of missiles supplied by Syria and Iran. Like an ostrich with its head in the sand, Israel's leaders have sat back and done nothing while Hezbollah has boldly positioned itself along the northern border of Israel.

At this writing, the perception of Israeli weakness has brought forth a daily shower of deadly missiles launched from Hezbollah strongholds in Lebanon. During the Lebanon war of 2006, more than a million Israelis were either living in bomb shelters or had been forced to flee southward to other cities in order to find safety and shelter.

Retreat, surrender, and the trading of land for peace have brought forth war in northern Israel and war in southern Israel. This has all come about because Israel's leaders are like those who lived in the days of Jeremiah.

> *Woe to the shepherds who destroy and scatter the flocks of My pasture! says the Lord. Therefore, so says the Lord G-d of Israel concerning the shepherds: You who pasture My people, you have scattered My flocks and have driven them away and have not taken care of them; behold, I will visit upon you the evil of your deeds, says the Lord.*

Because of the prophets my heart is broken within me, my bones shake, I was like a drunken man and like a man whom wine has overcome, because of the Lord and because of His holy words. For the land is full of adulterers, for because of oaths the land mourns, the dwellings in the wilderness are dried out, and their eagerness was evil and their power not right. For both prophet and priest are false; even in My house have I found their evil, says the Lord....

And in the prophets of Samaria I saw unseemliness; they prophesied by Baal and misled My people Israel. And in the prophets of Jerusalem I saw a horrible thing, committing adultery and going with falseness, and they encouraged evil-doers, that none returns from his evil; all of them were to Me as Sodom and her inhabitants as Gomorrah. Therefore, so said the Lord of Hosts concerning the prophets: Behold I will feed them wormwood and give them poisonous water to drink, for from the prophets of Jerusalem has falseness emanated to the whole land. So said the Lord of Hosts: Do not hearken to the words of the prophets who prophesy for you; they mislead you. The vision of their heart they speak, not from the mouth of the Lord. They say to those who despise Me, "The Lord has spoken, 'You shall have peace,'" and [to] everyone who follows the view of his heart they say, "No evil shall befall you." For who stood in the council of the Lord and will see and hear His word? He who hearkened to His word and listened. Behold a storm from the Lord has gone forth [with] fury, yea, a whirling storm, on the heads of the wicked it shall rest. The Lord's anger shall not return until He executes it and until He fulfills the plans of His heart. At the end of days, you shall consider it perfectly (Jeremiah 23:1–2;9–11;13–20).

DISENGAGEMENT FROM LEBANON

In 2000, the Prime Minister of Israel removed the Israeli army from South Lebanon and established a defensive line along Israel's northern border. Israelis were assured that if they left Lebanon and returned to their own borders, the Lebanese government would be free to disarm Hezbollah and assert control over the border area, thereby neutralizing the threat of terrorism.

What was the result? Iran and Syria quickly moved to support Hezbollah politically, financially, and militarily. Over the ensuing six years they recruited and trained an integrated network of Hezbollah militia that firmly entrenched its positions all along Israel's northern border. Steadily and methodically Hezbollah's patrons increased its weapons inventory to the point where an estimated 13,000 rockets stood capable of being launched against Israel's major northern cities.

With Iranian funds and Syrian support, Hezbollah built an integrated network of underground sites wherein rockets were both stored and readied for launch against innocent Israeli civilians. At frequent intervals, the fast-moving missiles with their deadly payload of high explosive wrapped in steel ball-bearings were surfaced and quickly launched. Many of these sites were strategically located in the midst of Lebanon's major population centers so as to make it impossible for Israel to take them out without killing large numbers of Lebanese civilians. Some sites extended as deep as 40 feet into the earth and were reinforced with concrete so that Israel's air force would experience great difficulty in locating and destroying them. This strategy proved very effective and to a large degree nullified Israel's traditional air superiority.

These underground storage and launching sites were interconnected by a series of impressive tunnels so that men and rockets could be easily moved from one location to another. Hezbollah guerillas would fire their missiles from one location and disappear below ground, only to rise again later to fire from a completely different location.

Israeli military planning and intelligence were sorely lacking. Basic necessities such as food and water, along with crucial items such as the tactical field maps showing the location of underground bunkers, mind fields, and the like, were largely unavailable to the troops that had been sent into Lebanon to wage war.

The six primary complaints the reserve soldiers raised after the war were:

1. Soldiers didn't have the proper training, equipment, weapons, food and water, and battlefield intelligence necessary to enable them to fight effectively.

2. They were often prevented from fighting.

3. Because of insufficient practice with their weapons before entering the war, they could not sight in their rifles accurately.

4. They hadn't been given thermal night vision devices, which the IDF had in stock and which Hezbollah successfully deployed in the field.

5. They didn't have adequate supplies of ammunition and communication equipment.

6. They lacked up-to-date aerial maps, which arrived only toward the end of the war.

Because Hezbollah had been preparing for the war ever since Israel's pullout from South Lebanon in 2000, they were able to continue launching missile salvos into Israeli cities for more than a month, including right up to the moment the cease-fire took effect.

Within days of the war's inception, the civilian population of northern Israel had come to understand that Israel's proud and vaunted leaders simply had no viable defense against the well-entrenched enemy that threatened the north with destruction. Poor intelligence led to an underestimation of the combat capabilities and tenacity of the Hezbollah fighters, as well as their ability to defend the areas from which they were launching their rockets.

In the third week of the war Israel belatedly began to commit meaningful ground forces, but indecision and the fear of negative international reaction caused further delays and missteps.

Consequently, the rockets continued to rain down on Israeli cities with no letup.

Incredibly, more than 4,000 rockets had fallen on Israeli cities and citizens before a halt to the fighting was announced. Due to intense political pressure exerted upon Israel by the nations of the world, the terms of the "cease-fire" virtually guaranteed a stunning victory for Hezbollah. For Israel's enemies the long wait had finally ended amidst the declarations of the world's media that Israel could be defeated on the battlefield. *The Economist* magazine declared on the cover of its August 19, 2006 edition, "Nasrallah Wins the War!"

For weeks, young Israeli soldiers had fought desperate hand-to-hand battles with Hezbollah regulars, proving their bravery and dedication beyond all measure. In no way should there be any doubt that the soldiers of the Israeli army did not seek to carry out the task of fighting this war. The problem did not lie with them. Instead, it rested firmly on the shoulders of those leaders who in the end moved to engineer the retreat from Lebanon. These same leaders had, in the same manner, engineered the retreat from Gaza less than a year before.

Many people believe the Lebanese Army, augmented by an international peacekeeping force, will be able to successfully enforce the cease-fire only until Iran, Syria, and Hezbollah decide to start the next round. Realistically speaking, however, the UN will never be able to bring lasting peace because the Lebanese army has no intention of disarming Hezbollah, and the international force has not been directed to do so either. This farce of a plan will soon result in a triumphant Hezbollah, aided and abetted by Iran and Syria, once again establishing itself as power broker in southern Lebanon, free to resume the rebuilding of its terror inventory in preparation for the next conflict with Israel.

Hezbollah, Syria, and Iran will undoubtedly utilize the "cease-fire" to re-arm the Hezbollah war machine to ever greater levels of sophistication and effectiveness, preparing for the next war, when the rockets will have a much longer range, much larger payloads, and much more sophisticated guidance systems.

WHERE IS THE G-D OF ISRAEL?

From the beginning of the war, something was woefully lacking in the corridors of power in Jerusalem. There was absolutely no spiritual leadership exhibited or spoken of by Israel's leaders. The G-d of Israel was nowhere to be found. He was not in the public speeches or statements of the Prime Minister or the Ministry of Defense, nor was a single word spoken regarding the need to seek His wisdom, His strategy, and His mercy. None dared call upon His mighty name to fight for Israel.

This was a war in which Israel's leaders chose to look to their own wisdom and strength (with a bit of Israeli air power thrown in), rather than to Him who declares that it is by His mighty hand and outstretched arm that Israel is victorious on the battlefield. All were surprised when victory did not come to Israel, to its air force, to its political and religious leaders, or to the people of the land, who were forced to live like insects in bomb shelters in order to preserve their lives.

Until the cease-fire took place, all of Israel's military might, from its mighty air force to the brave foot soldiers on the ground, could not stop the missiles from raining down on Israel's cities and citizens.

BUT FOR THE GRACE OF G-D!

The war held a small silver lining, however, even though the world and the Israeli media portrayed it as a great victory for Nasrallah. For in reality, the Israeli Air Force and the IDF had inflicted great damage on the Hezbollah forces. The G-d of Israel in His mercy and grace had once again remembered and fought for His people and their men of war against their enemies.

TURN TO ME AND BE SAVED DECLARES THE G-D OF ISRAEL

What Israel needs so desperately after this war is not more F-16 aircraft, Apache helicopters, or weapons from America. Rather, Israel's leaders and the whole house of Israel need to humble themselves and return to our G-d; to cry out for forgiveness before our G-d and to seek His face, His strategy, His mercy, His salvation, and deliverance.

> *"Declare and present, let them even take counsel together; who announced this from before, [who] declared it from then? Is it not I, the Lord, and there are no other gods besides Me, a just and saving G-d there is not besides Me. Turn to Me and be saved, all the ends of the earth, for I am G-d, and there is no other. By Myself I swore, righteousness emanated from My mouth, a word, and it shall not be retracted, that to Me shall every knee kneel, every tongue shall swear." But to me did He say by the Lord righteousness and strength, to Him shall come and be ashamed all who are incensed against Him. Through the Lord shall all the seed of Israel find righteousness and boast* (Isaiah 45:21–25).

Yet despite the above promise, Israel's leaders and people have chosen to remain apart from the G-d who even now yearns to embrace them and bring them to full repentance and restoration. Stubborn Israel still refuses to bow the knee to the only One who has the power to save and to heal, not realizing that by placing their faith in the edicts of men rather than the promises of G-d they consign themselves to eternal failure and disappointment. Israel's leaders have chosen to follow their own wisdom, which means doing that which is right in their own eyes. The fruit of this foolish and misguided thinking is today made manifest in the form of raining death by missile attack, a first-ever IDF defeat on the ground, and the certainty of future conflict with an emboldened Hezbollah and its patrons.

WHAT ARE WE FIGHTING FOR?

To the astonishment of most Israelis, the Prime Minister held a press conference during the third week of the Lebanese war and announced publicly that victory in the war in Lebanon would advance his plan to withdraw from Judea and

Samaria. Soldiers, parents, and politicians of all persuasions were stunned by his remarks.

After giving up Gaza, all Israel had been told by Ariel Sharon and his government that peace and security had finally been established on Israel's southern border. Mere months later, what had been the result? Hamas had come to power in Gaza and rockets had begun raining down on Israel's southern towns and cities. Now, in the midst of the Lebanese war, the Prime Minister of Israel was saying publicly to all of the soldiers who were fighting and dying, and specifically to those who had left Judea and Samaria to join the battle, "When the war is over you will have no home or land to come back to."

Many Israeli soldiers from Judea and Samaria were asking the question: "What are we fighting for?" While it was the right question to ask, there would be no plausible answer from the government.

I WILL SET ISRAEL'S FINAL BORDERS!

Just before winning the 2006 election, the current Prime Minister of Israel made an interesting declaration: "I will set Israel's final borders!"

When I heard this, I thought to myself, "Really?"

The G-d of Israel has authored a word from the Tanach that the Prime Minister should consider very carefully before acting on his plan to give over Israel's promised inheritance in Judea and Samaria. The Lord has some questions for the one who declares, "I will set Israel's final borders!" The Lord indeed has some questions for the one who has declared he will give over Israel's promised inheritance to a foreign god—Allah.

> Then the Lord answered Job from the tempest and said, "Who is this who gives dark counsel, with words, without knowledge? Now gird your loins like a man, and I will ask you and [you] tell Me. Where were you when I

founded the earth? Tell if you know understanding. Who placed its measures if you know, or who extended a line over it? On what were its sockets sunk, or who laid its cornerstone? When the morning stars sing together, and all the angels of G-d shout?...

"In [all] *your days, did you command the morning? Did you tell the dawn its place? To grasp the corners of the earth so that the wicked shall be shaken from it?...*

"Have the gates of death been revealed to you, and do you see the gates of the shadow of death? Do you understand [everything] *until the breadths of the earth? Tell if you know it all"* (Job 38:1–7;12–13;17–18).

Sometime soon the G-d of Israel is going to demand an answer to these questions from the one who boasted in his arrogance, "I will be the one who sets Israel's final borders!"

In chapters 40–48 of the book of Ezekiel, we find conclusive proof that only the G-d of Israel will set Israel's final borders, and they are going to be significantly greater than anyone has envisioned as of today.

DISENGAGEMENT FROM GAZA

One year prior to the Israeli-Lebanon war, then–Prime Minister Ariel Sharon and his government forcibly removed 10,000 Jews from their inheritance in Gaza. Many Israelis supported the disengagement, believing it would bring peace and security.

The Israeli media and intellectuals touted it as the way to bring reconciliation to the region and looked to it as the first step in the birth of an independent Palestinian State. What was the result of the disengagement?

GAZA: A DISENGAGEMENT FROM REALITY AND TRUTH

Lieutenant-General (ret.) Moshe Ya'alon, IDF Chief of Staff until the implementation of the Gaza withdrawal was recently quoted in an interview as saying, "It was a disengagement from reality and a disengagement from the truth."

"The process created an illusionary hope," Ya'alon said, "which was not planned strategically and practically. The disengagement was mainly a media spin. Those who initiated it and led it lacked the strategic, security, political, and historical background. They were image counselors and spin doctors. These people put Israel into a virtual spin, disconnected from reality, using a media spin campaign which is imploding before our eyes."

"There is no doubt that the disengagement failed," Ya'alon said. The entire withdrawal and expulsion of 10,000 Jewish residents from Gaza and northern Samaria "was an internal Israeli game that ignored what's going on outside Israel."

The former Chief of Staff does not accept the argument that because polls have shown a broad section of the Israeli public wanted to leave Gaza, it was the right thing to do. "The Israeli public backed the disengagement because it was blinded and drugged and because it really wanted to free itself from the burden of the conflict and divide the land....We shouldn't fool ourselves. We live in the Middle East. We cannot barricade ourselves behind walls and fences. There is no such thing as unilateralism. Even when we refuse to talk with our neighbors there is interaction with them."

The former Chief of Staff says that Gaza has been allowed to become a staging ground for the worst of the terror groups taking part in the global jihad. "At the moment, our situation in Gaza is similar to southern Lebanon," he said. "Plenty of arms have been smuggled into Gaza: explosives, Katyusha rockets, anti-aircraft rockets, anti-tank rockets, Grad rockets. As a result of the manner in which the pullout was carried out, there are [Hezbollah], Al-Qaeda and Iranian elements in the Gaza Strip."

"When the steps are withdrawal after withdrawal after withdrawal, we convey weakness," Ya'alon concludes. "And he who conveys weakness in the Middle East is like a weak animal in nature: he comes under attack."[1]

BROKEN PROMISES, LIES, AND DECEPTION

Since the unilateral withdrawal from Gaza, ten thousand people have lost their homes, their land, their inheritance, their livelihood, their schools, their synagogues, and everything they had worked for all their lives. The government promised them compensation. What did they receive? For months on end they received only broken promises and lies.

Thousands were forced to live in hotel rooms, schools, and tents, with no money, no work, no land, and no hope. Many were promised compensation for their homes and businesses, which had been destroyed by the Israeli army, itself sworn to protect Israeli citizens. Incredibly, they did not receive the promised compensation, and many were forced to continue paying mortgages on homes that no longer existed!

The government of Ariel Sharon made no meaningful plans or provisions for the ten thousand productive citizens of Gaza. Overnight, the government turned them into homeless refugees—victims of broken promises, lies, and deception. Energetic and productive people who were growing flowers, fruits, and vegetables that brought millions of dollars a year in foreign exchange into Israel were reduced to homeless wards of the state.

The great human tragedy of the expulsion from Gaza was not only that ten thousand Jews were expelled from their homes, but that they were expelled from their way of life as well. No doubt the very heart of G-d Himself was broken as He looked down from Heaven and witnessed the awful spectacle of Jew against Jew, brother against brother, as one by one the families were dragged from their homes by police who had been specially trained for one objective only—to remove them from the land!

Many Israelis were incited by the government, the media, and certain politicians to hate their brothers and sisters who had been expelled from Gaza, portraying them as troublemakers and criminals who stood in the way of the enlightened plan for peace. Perhaps these haters should consider the events of the Lebanese war in light of what Joseph's brothers said to each other when they stood before their own brother whom they had sold into slavery in Egypt.

> *And they said to one another, "Indeed, we are guilty for our brother, that we witnessed the distress of his soul when he begged us, and we did not listen. That is why this trouble has come upon us"* (Genesis 42:21).

When will we Israelis who are surrounded by a billion Muslims, many of whom hate and revile us, and who daily seek our death and destruction, ever fully understand what a terrible sin it is to hate our own brothers and sisters simply because they lived their lives in accordance with G-d's promises to them?

We Israeli Jews must come to understand that we are one people and one nation, who have one G-d, and what happens to the least of us will one day be visited upon us all simply because we are all Jews. We are 13 million people on a planet with more than 6 billion souls. By the mercy of almighty G-d we have been given a very tiny piece of land as a promised homeland after more than 1,900 years of dispersion. If we allow men or governments to set us against each other so they can divide our land and give it over to a foreign god, know for certain that the destiny of those who were expelled from their land for the sake of a false peace will one day fall upon those who supported their expulsion because we are one people who are as inseparably tied together to the land, as we are to the G-d who promised it to us.

"PEACE, PEACE," WHEN THERE IS NO PEACE

Where is the promised peace that Ariel Sharon and his associates promised the Israeli public which supported their "disengagement plan"? Instead of peace, what has come forth from the disengagement?

First, we witnessed the rise to political power in Gaza of Hamas, a violent terrorist organization that has sworn to destroy the nation of Israel.

Second, we experienced the fear and terror of raining death as Palestinian terrorists moved their missile launchers to the northernmost borders of Gaza and began to lob volley after volley of missiles into Israeli cities that were now easily within their range.

Third, we have witnessed numerous attacks against Israeli soldiers, along with kidnappings and the usual terror and violence.

Fourth, there has been a direct link established between Hamas and Iran, just as there now exists a direct link between Iran and Hezbollah.

Consequently, Iran has the ability to attack Israel by proxy using Hezbollah in the north and Hamas in the south. Under constant pressure from America to create a Palestinian State, Israel has allowed the creation of "Hamastan" on its southern border. The same policy of retreat and surrender has led to the creation of "Hezbollahstan" on its northern border. Without a doubt it will not be long before Hezbollah, with the backing of Syria and Iran, will seek to topple the existing Lebanese government and seize the reins of political power to control all of Lebanon and to create another terrorist state in the Middle East.

WE WILL BUILD A WALL AND PLASTER IT WITH MORTAR!

The strategy behind the disengagement is based upon Israeli separation from the Palestinian people by a wall being constructed in various parts of the West Bank and Jerusalem. One must ask the question: Have we Israelis learned nothing over the last few months of war and terror? Have we not learned that missiles have absolutely no problem going over walls no matter how high they are?

Interestingly, the Tanach prophesied just such a time when Israel and its leaders would seek to build a wall and plaster it with lies and deception, saying "Peace, peace," when there is no peace!

> *"Son of man, prophesy against the prophets of Israel who prophesy, and say to those who prophesy out of their own hearts: Hearken to the word of the Lord. So said the Lord G-d: Woe is to the mad prophets who follow their desire and what they have not seen. Like foxes in ruins were your prophets, O Israel. You have not gone up into the breaches nor have you built a fence for the house of Israel, to stand in war on the day of the Lord"* (Ezekiel 13:2–5).

Just as it was prophesied long ago, Israel's leaders and prophets are not listening to the word of the Lord; rather, they are choosing to do what is right in their own eyes. They have not gone into the breaches, nor have they built a wall of faith and trust in their G-d around the house of Israel. They are choosing instead to build a wall of bricks, plastering it with lies and deception that cannot possibly stand in the battle on the day of the Lord.

> *Therefore, so said the Lord G-d: Since you spoke falsehoods and prophesied lies, therefore, behold I am against you, says the Lord G-d. And My hand shall be against the prophets who prophesy vanity and the diviners of lies; in the counsel of My people they shall not be, and in the roster of the house of Israel they shall not be inscribed, and to the land of Israel they shall not come, and you will know that I am the Lord G-d* (Ezekiel 13:8–9).

The Lord is declaring that when Israel's leaders speak, it will be a lie and a falsehood when they say, "Build a wall, give up your land, forsake your inheritance, and then there will be peace." Therefore, because our leaders have spoken lies of their own making, behold the Lord declares, "I the Lord am against you!"

What a profoundly terrifying prophetic word from the G-d of Israel to the leaders of Israel. Because of their lies, their names will not be written down in the register of the house of Israel, nor will they be allowed to enter or remain in the land of Israel when the Messiah rules and reigns.

G-d's hand will be against them for one reason—because they have said "Peace" when there is no peace!

BECAUSE THEY HAVE SAID PEACE WHEN THERE IS NO PEACE

Because, indeed because they misled My people, saying, "Peace," when there is no peace, and it is building a flimsy wall, and behold they are plastering it with daub. Say to the plasterers with daub, "Behold, it will fall. If there will be driving rain, then you, gigantic hailstones, will fall, and a storm wind will crack [it]. And behold, the wall has fallen! Will it not be said to you, 'Where is the plaster that you have plastered?'" Therefore, so said the Lord G-d: I will cause a storm wind to crack [the wall] with My fury, and there shall be a driving rain with My wrath, and gigantic hailstones with fury to destroy [it]. And I shall demolish the wall that you plastered with daub, and I shall make it reach the ground, and its foundation will be bared, and it will fall, and you will perish in its midst, and you will know that I am the Lord. And I shall spend My fury on the wall and on those who plaster it with daub, and I shall say to you, "The wall is not here, neither are those who plaster it" (Ezekiel 13:10–15).

The Lord declares the time would come when Israel's leaders would seek to mislead His people saying "Peace" when there is no peace. That time has arrived, beginning in earnest with the Oslo Peace Process and continuing with the withdrawal from Lebanon in 2000 and the disengagement from Gaza in 2005. This great lie and deception has now extended into the twenty-first century, when Israel's leaders began to build a wall to separate themselves from the Palestinians saying, "We will surrender our inheritance in Judea and Samaria and retreat behind our wall in order to have peace."

WHAT IS THE WHITEWASH?

What is the whitewash (daub) they used as plaster for their wall? It is the whitewash of lies, deception, and their power to lead the people astray. Yet the Lord G-d of Israel declares, "The wall will fall so that its foundation of lies will be laid bare, and the leaders and prophets of Israel who plastered the wall and whitewashed [daubed] it with lies and deception saying peace when there is no peace, will be consumed in its midst and will be no more."

This is a powerful prophetic word for Israel's political and spiritual leaders today. It is a powerful word for those in Israel's media who have espoused peace, surrender, and retreat. It is a powerful prophetic word for you to know and understand as well, because the consequences of this policy of whitewash and lies are going to impact your life, the lives of your family, and all those living in the nation of Israel. All would do well to heed and understand G-d's prophetic word for a time such as this.

WILL YOU BE DECEIVED?

What's coming next for Israel? Each of us will be forced to choose and take a stand on the issue of giving over the "mountains of Israel," Judea and Samaria, to a foreign god—Allah.

The Tanach has declared there is an evil time coming: a time of great deception and lies from the leaders and prophets of Israel. They will build a wall and willingly offer to give over their inheritance in Judea and Samaria to those who worship a foreign god. They will build a wall and retreat behind it, promising peace, but peace will never come.

Israel's leaders seek to join other world leaders and politicians in declaring peace and security, but there will be no peace or security. They will seek to enlist the media's help in every way in promoting their plan to deceive the people into giving up their G-d-promised inheritance in the mountains of Israel. They will seek to build a wall and divide our land, all in the name of a false peace.

THE RECONCILIATION OF THE PA AND HAMAS

It is possible that there will be some kind of public reconciliation between Hamas and the Palestinian Authority, for both recognize that they can never achieve their common goal of a Palestinian state unless they work together.

No matter what form or shape this reconciliation takes, they will make false statements and take positions that have no bearing in truth or reality. Their initial purpose will be to restore funding from the E.U. and America so they can arm themselves and pay for their armies. Their primary goal will be to bring pressure upon America and the E.U. to force Israel into ceding Judea, Samaria, and east Jerusalem for the creation of a Palestinian state.

They will undoubtedly use smooth language that tacitly acknowledges Israel's right to exist—until they are ready to destroy it. They will espouse peace, as will Israel's leaders, America, the E.U., and the UN. But in the end Hamas and the Palestinian Authority will conspire with Syria, Iran, and Hezbollah to bring about a coordinated attack with one goal—the complete destruction of Israel.

Over time, as the relentless pressure from America and the E.U. mounts, Israel's political leaders may find themselves once again seeking to remove—in the name of a false peace— tens of thousands of Israelis from Judea and Samaria—the "mountains of Israel."

Just as with the disengagement from Gaza, they will seek to use their political and economic power to force people to capitulate or face financial ruin. They will use every lever of power at their disposal to bring about the successful completion of their plan to divide Israel and give it into the hands of a foreign god. They will do it in the name of peace, but it will bring G-d's judgment on Israel and His wrath upon her leaders and prophets.

Make no mistake about it. Part of the false peace agreement will include a push to cede east Jerusalem to the Hamas/Palestinian Authority entity as the capital for its new nation. Above all else, Hamas, the Palestinians, and the Arab-Muslim nations will demand and seek to make Jerusalem the capital of the new Palestinian State.

JUDGMENT OF THE NATIONS

We have written before that the division of the land of Israel will bring about G-d's wrath on all the nations who cause this event to take place. It is no small matter in the eyes of the G-d of Israel. While the Lord seems to have put Olmert's plan to give over Judea and Samaria on the shelf in the wake of the Lebanese debacle, the issue remains like a pregnant woman waiting to give birth. We know from G-d's word that the land of Israel will be divided by the nations. So it is not a question of *if* the land will be divided; rather, it is *when* it will be divided!

> *For behold, in those days and in that time when I return the captivity of Judah and Jerusalem, I will gather all the nations and I will take them down to the Valley of Jehoshaphat, and I will contend with them there concerning My people and My heritage, Israel, which they scattered among the nations, and My land they divided* (Joel 4:1–2).

Woe to the nations and leaders who "divided My land among themselves," says the Lord G-d of Israel! Woe to those who agree to an evil scheme. Woe to the leaders of Israel who would say "Peace, peace," and willingly divide their G-d-promised land for a false promise.

EACH OF US MUST MAKE A DECISION

You must make a choice whether to stand with G-d or against Him. There will be no middle ground on this issue. Make no mistake about it. G-d's wrath will be poured onto those who divide His land and on all those who join with them to plaster the wall with lies.

> *Therefore, so said the Lord G-d: I will cause a storm wind to crack* [the wall] *with My fury, and there shall be a driving rain with My wrath, and gigantic hailstones with fury to destroy* [it] (Ezekiel 13:13).

We don't have to wonder what G-d's wrath looks like. All you have to do is look at the long history of Israel's disobedience toward G-d, and you will understand just how thorough G-d's wrath is.

Remember, the northern kingdom of Israel rebelled against the G-d of Israel and was given into the hand of the king of Assyria who took many as slaves. The northern kingdom of Israel subsequently ceased to exist—that's what G-d's wrath looks like!

THE FORK IN THE ROAD

The G-d of Israel has brought His people and His nation to a fork in the road. We and our leaders must choose to go either to the left or to the right. We must choose to take the road that says "G-d's way" or the one that says "Man's way." We must choose between blessings and curses, for in so doing we are choosing either life or death.

Which road will you choose to take—blessings or curses? Know for certain your choice will have eternal consequences. What will you do? What will all Israel do? Will it be as it was in the time of Elijah the prophet?

> *And Elijah drew near to all the people and said, "Until when are you hopping between two ideas? If the Lord is G-d, go after Him, and if the Baal, go after him." And the people did not answer him a word* (1 Kings 18:21).

Will we once again be like Israel when the Lord called Jeremiah the prophet to speak to them about their rebellion against their G-d?

OBEY MY VOICE, AND I WILL BE YOUR G-D,
AND YOU WILL BE MY PEOPLE

For neither did I speak with your forefathers nor did I command them on the day I brought them out of the land of Egypt, concerning a burnt offering or a sacrifice. But this thing did I command them, saying: Obey Me so that I am your G-d and you are My people, and you walk in all the ways that I command you, so that it may be well with you. But they did not obey nor did they incline their ear, but walked according to [their] *own counsels and in the view of their evil heart, and they went backwards and not forwards. Since the day that your fathers came forth out of the land of Egypt until this day, I sent you all My servants the prophets, sending them day* [after day] *with every fresh morn. Yet they hearkened not to Me nor did they incline their ear, but stiffened their necks; they did worse than their fathers. And when you will speak all of these words to them and they will not hearken to you, and you call to them and they will not answer you, Then say to them: This is the nation that did not hear the voice of the Lord their G-d and has not received correction; out of their mouth faithfulness has disappeared, yea rooted out!* (Jeremiah 7:22–28)

ENDNOTE

1. ArutzSheva July 06, 2006 Former Chief of Staff: Sharon's Disengagement a Disaster—Ezra Ha Levi.

Chapter Five

THE PRINCE OF PERSIA

O G-d, have no silence, do not be silent and do not be still, O G-d (Psalm 83:2).

G-D SPEAKS FROM HIS WORD TO THE WORLD TODAY

Ireland's National Museum announced in July 2006 that a 1,200-year-old Book of Psalms, discovered by a construction worker in a bog, was comparable in archaeological significance to "an Irish equivalent to the Dead Sea Scrolls." The discovery of the ancient Psalter was said by museum officials to be remarkable for two reasons—first, it survived so long in boggy terrain; and second, it was spotted by a construction worker, who halted a mechanical digger just in time to save it from destruction.[1]

Most noteworthy about the discovery of this ancient manuscript was that it was open to Psalm 83, written more than 3,000 years ago and witness to what could easily be the headlines for any major newspaper, magazine, or television program today. This ancient Psalm declares that the enemies of the G-d of Israel will make an uproar among the nations and that those who hate Him will greatly exalt themselves.

They said, "Come, let us destroy them from [being] a nation, and the name of Israel will no longer be remembered."

For they have taken counsel with one accord; against You they form a pact. The tents of Edom and the Ishmaelites, Moab and the Hagrites; Gebal, Ammon, and Amalek, Philistia with the inhabitants of Tyre. Also Assyria joined them; they were the arm of the children of Lot forever (Psalm 83:5–9).

The president of Iran certainly fits this description perfectly. He has truly made an uproar among the nations, declaring that nothing and no one is going to stop him from acquiring nuclear weapons. He has also stated clearly that it is his intention to destroy both Israel and America. He has openly proclaimed to the world's news media his plans against the G-d of Israel and the Jewish people—to wipe them off the map of the earth!

Psalm 83 prophesies a conspiracy among the nations that surround Israel, an evil and diabolical covenant that they should work together for the sole purpose of destroying its very memory: "Come, let us destroy them from [being] a nation, and the name of Israel will no longer be remembered." Today, the words and public pronouncements *of both the leader of Iran and the leader of Hezbollah in Lebanon* mingle with the echoes of previous utterances by the elder Assad of Syria against Israel and the Jewish people, mirroring almost verbatim the prophetic words written thousands of years ago in Psalm 83. Let there be no doubt—the Lord is speaking prophetically to both Israel and the nations through this Psalm.

Notice that the Psalmist used the words "Let us destroy them from [being] a nation."

Remember that ancient Israel was destroyed by the Romans in 70 C.E. and that for over 1,900 years the Jewish people wandered throughout the earth in exile. Yet by the mighty hand of G-d, modern Israel took its place among the nations of the world in 1948. Because there is no record of any alliance such as that described in the verses having taken place in biblical times against Israel, one must therefore understand these verses as having been written for today, when Israel once again exists as a nation, surrounded by enemies possessing the will and the means to attack and destroy her.

Interestingly, the Psalm prophetically lists the names of some of the ancient nations who have entered into this covenant. The nations listed are primarily the nations that surround Israel today. Since 1948, these nations have launched a series of wars with one purpose in mind—to wipe Israel out as a nation.

For the Lord G-d does nothing unless He has revealed His secret to His servants, the prophets (Amos 3:7).

This prophecy, written thousands of years ago, is coming alive today. It is virtually jumping off the pages of the Psalms.

PROPHECY FROM OLD APPLIED TO OUR TIME

During the days of Daniel, King Nebuchadnezzar of Babylon came and destroyed Jerusalem and took the Jews captive to Babylon for a period of 70 years. It was during Daniel's time in the kingdom of Babylon that he had a vision from G-d in regard to the future of the Jewish people.

DANIEL IS TERRIFIED BY A VISION

In the first year of Cyrus, king of Persia, a word was revealed to Daniel, who was named Belteshazzar, and the word was true, and for a long time, and he understood the word and he understood it in the vision. In those days, I, Daniel, had been mourning for three weeks of days. I ate no white bread, neither did meat nor wine enter my mouth, and I did not anoint myself until the completion of three weeks of days. And on the twenty-fourth day of the first month, when I was beside the great river, the Tigris. I lifted my eyes and saw, and behold a man clad in linen, and his loins were girded with a girdle of gold studded with jewels. And his body was like tarshish, and his face was like the appearance of lightning, and his eyes were like firebrands, and his

arms and his legs were like the appearance of bran-
dished copper, and the sound of his words was like the
voice of a multitude. And I, Daniel, alone saw the vi-
sion, but the men who were with me did not see the vi-
sion, but a great quaking fell upon them, and they fled
into hiding. But I remained alone, and I saw this great
vision, and no strength was left within me, and my
complexion was turned in me into corruption, and I
could not summon up strength. Then I heard the voice
of his words, and when I heard the voice of his words, I
fell into a sound sleep on my face, and my face was to
the ground (Daniel 10:1–9).

Daniel received a vision that terrified him to the point where he had no strength. In the vision he lifted up his eyes and saw a "man" dressed in linen, whose waist was girded with a belt of pure gold. His body was like beryl, his face had the appearance of lightning, and his eyes were like firebrands. His arms and legs were like the gleam of polished copper, and the sound of his words like the voice of a multitude.

Daniel was not alone when he saw this vision, and a great quaking fell upon the men that were with him as they ran away to hide themselves. Can you imagine the power of this vision? The men with Daniel felt a spirit of dread from something they could not see, a spirit so strong that they fled in abject terror and hid themselves in fear for their lives.

When Daniel heard the sound of the words from this man dressed in linen, the natural color of his face turned a deathly pallor, and he fell to the ground on his face in a deep sleep. Daniel saw this man dressed in white linen again when the angel Michael gave him greater revelation about the time of Jacob's distress.

And I, Daniel, saw, and behold two others were stand-
ing, one on this side of the river bank, and one on that
side of the riverbank. And he said to the man clad in
linen, who was above the waters of the river, "How long
will it be until the secret end?" And I heard the man
clad in linen, who was above the waters of the river, and

he raised his right hand and his left hand to the heavens, and he swore by the Life of the world, that in the time of [two] times and a half, and when they have ended shattering the strength of the holy people, all these will end (Daniel 12:5–7).

The man clothed in white linen declares to Daniel exactly when the power of the evil king of the Fourth Kingdom described in Daniel chapter 7 will be broken. After the time of (two) times, and a half (three and one half years), and when they have ended shattering the strength of the holy people, all these will end!

Who could this one clothed in white linen be? Remember, in Daniel chapter 7 he was taken up to Heaven in a vision and he saw the Ancient of Days sitting on His holy throne with thousands upon thousands ministering before Him. Then one like the Son of Man appeared before Him, and to Him was given a kingdom, dominion, and authority to rule and reign. I believe this is the Messiah who is to come, and He appeared to Daniel to give him revelation and understanding about the fate of the Jewish people in the latter days, at the end of the time of Jacob's distress.

DANIEL COMFORTED

And behold, a hand touched me and moved me on my knees and the palms of my hands. And he said to me, "Daniel, man of desirable qualities, contemplate the words I speak to you and stand upright, for now I have been sent to you." And when he spoke to me this word, I stood quaking. And he said to me "Fear not, Daniel, for since the first day that you set your heart to contemplate and to fast before your G-d, your words were heard, and I have come because of your words. And the prince of the kingdom of Persia has been standing against me for twenty-one days, and behold Michael, one of the first princes, has come to help, and I remained there beside the kings of Persia" (Daniel 10:10–13).

The Tanach reveals that a hand touched Daniel and set him trembling on his hands and knees and that an angel spoke to him with great and comforting words saying, "O Daniel, man of high esteem, understand the words that I am about to tell you and stand upright, for I have been sent to you."

The angel addresses Daniel as a man of "desirable qualities." Can you imagine an angel of G-d addressing you as a "person of desirable qualities?" What an incredible blessing it must have been for Daniel to have heard that greeting.

The Tanach reveals that this angel was sent to Daniel by the G-d of Israel in answer to Daniel's fervent and persistent prayers for his people. What a testimony and example Daniel is for us today. He was a man who would not cease praying until he received an answer from G-d.

A great deal can be learned here about the power and importance of prayer. Daniel had been fasting and praying for 21 days when an angel of the Lord revealed to him, "I have been sent to you in answer to your fervent and persistent prayers to give you understanding."

Daniel prayed expecting to hear from G-d. He prayed believing G-d would answer him, and he was not about to cease persevering before the Lord until he received an answer from G-d. When we humble ourselves and seek the Lord, delayed answers often mean we must press in even more fervently until we have heard from Him.

Our prayers often have to pass through enemy territory, and we must be willing to pray as Daniel prayed until the Lord answers our prayers.

Do you pray like Daniel? Do you expect and believe G-d will answer your prayers? When Daniel prayed, it touched G-d's heart. When you pray does it touch the heart of G-d?

Daniel believed that the time of Israel's captivity in Babylon was about to end, and he was seeking G-d's plan for His people. Daniel prayed, believing that the fate of his nation and his people depended on his prayers. Daniel was seeking to know

G-d's eternal plan for His people. G-d had eternity in mind when Daniel was praying, and that is why He revealed to him His plan for the Jewish people in the latter days.

WHO IS THE PRINCE OF PERSIA?

We find in chapter 9 of Daniel that the angel Gabriel came to give him insight and understanding. Daniel had seen Gabriel before in a vision, so he recognized him and was not afraid. I believe that here again, it was the angel Gabriel who was specifically dispatched by G-d to give Daniel understanding of His plan for His people in the latter days.

Interestingly, the angel reveals to Daniel why he was not able to come to him immediately but was delayed for 21 days. He encourages Daniel not to be afraid and to understand that his prayers were heard by his G-d when he humbled himself before Him seeking wisdom and understanding.

Much is revealed here about praying expectantly. G-d heard Daniel's prayers and dispatched the angel Gabriel to give him an immediate answer to his prayers. Yet satan sent the prince of Persia, a principality, to withstand the angel Gabriel for 21 days. It is obvious from Gabriel's revelation to Daniel that the prince of Persia had the power to waylay him and keep him from reaching Daniel with the word from the Lord.

The prince of Persia is a demonic being who has great satanic power over a specific territory or area of the earth and its inhabitants. If we examine the map of the principality of Media and Persia we find that the area under the power and influence of the prince of Persia extends from modern day Iran and covers the entire territory of the modern day Middle East.

Today, just as in the days of Daniel, the prince of Persia exercises dominion and authority over the rulers and people of the Middle East. His power is consummately evil, and he is still operating today, as evidenced by the fulfillment of the prophetic words in Psalm 83.

Satan has empowered the prince of Persia to bring forth a leader in modern day Iran who is seeking to "wipe Israel off the map." Make no mistake about it, the current leadership of Iran is empowered by and completely under the influence of satanic powers, and in particular those of the prince of Persia.

The prophet Zechariah also prophesied about the territory of the prince of Persia, confirming Daniel's experience.

And the angel who was speaking to me came forth, and he said to me, "Now lift up your eyes and see what this is that is coming forth." And I said, "What is it?" And he said, "This is the ephah that is going forth." And he said, "This is [the punishment of those] *whose eye* [gazes] *over the entire land." And behold! A talent of lead was being lifted, and this one woman was sitting in the midst of the ephah. And he said, "This is Wickedness." And he cast her into the midst of the ephah, and he cast the lead weight into her mouth. And I lifted my eyes, and I saw—and behold!—two women were coming forth with wind in their wings, and they had wings like the wings of the stork. And they lifted up the ephah between the earth and the heaven. And I said to the angel who spoke to me, "Where are they taking the ephah?" And he said to me, "To build a house for it in the land of Shinar, and it will be prepared, and they shall place it there on its base"* (Zechariah 5:5–11).

In these prophetic verses we see that an unnamed angel spoke to Zechariah just as Gabriel spoke to Daniel. He told the prophet Zechariah to lift up his eyes and to declare what he saw going forth.

Zechariah saw a woman sitting inside the tub. When he asked what this represented, the angel said, "This is Wickedness," and the tub in which she is sitting is being taken to the land of Shinar to build for her a house, where she will be set on her own pedestal!

The land of Shinar is in modern day Iraq, ancient Babylon, and the "house of wickedness," which was established there by satan, is still in existence today. This evil power center or principality will someday be left to its own devices after the departure of the American forces. There can be little doubt that Iraq will thereafter align itself with the covenant of destruction against Israel.

REVELATION FROM G-D

"And I have come to enable you to understand what will happen to your people at the end of the days, for there is yet a vision for those days."

And when he spoke to me according to these words, I set my face to the ground, and I was dumbfounded. And behold [one] like the image of the sons of man was touching my lips, and I opened my mouth and spoke, and I said to the one standing opposite me, "My lord, in the vision my joints turned upon me, and I did not summon up strength. Now how will this servant of my lord be able to speak with this my lord?" And for me, from now on, strength will not stay in me, and a soul is not left in me.

And the one having the appearance like that of a man continued to touch me, and he strengthened me. And he said, "Fear not, man of desirable qualities; peace be to you, be strong and be strong," and when he spoke to me, I gained strength, and I said, "Let my lord speak, for you have strengthened me." And he said, "Do you know why I have come to you? And now I shall return to battle with the prince of Persia; then I shall leave, and behold the prince of Greece is coming. Indeed, I shall tell you what is inscribed in a true script, but no one strengthens himself concerning these matters except Michael, your prince" (Daniel 10:14–21).

Daniel is told by the angel that he has come to give him understanding of what will happen to the Jewish people in the latter days. Daniel was so completely overcome by the words of the angel that he turned his face to the ground and was speechless.

What a statement and revelation from the angel of the Lord to Daniel! Then the one who resembled sons of man touched his lips and Daniel was finally able to speak. Daniel was so overwhelmed by the presence of Lord that in his humility he said, "How can such a servant of my lord talk with such as my lord?"

Then the angel with a human appearance touched Daniel and strengthened him, and he said, "Fear not, man of desirable qualities; peace be to you; be strong and be strong!"

The angel's words were of incredible blessing and comfort to Daniel. What words of blessing and comfort they should be to each of us as we pray for Israel as well. Those who walk with the Lord and are able to hear His voice need not be afraid, for our G-d is with us to deliver us from the hand of our enemies. Daniel's prayers touched the heart of G-d, and that is why He came and manifested Himself to Daniel, commanding His angel to comfort and strengthen him.

I SHALL RETURN TO FIGHT AGAINST THE PRINCE OF PERSIA

Here the angel reveals where he must go after giving Daniel revelation and understanding—to "fight against the prince of Persia." Why would he have to fight against him? Because the prince of Persia would use every possible means of deception to cause the kings of that entire area to rise up and destroy the Jewish people.

CYRUS IS MY SHEPHERD!

What did the Lord do through Daniel? He allowed him to live into the first year of the reign of King Cyrus, who conquered Babylon. I believe that Daniel showed King Cyrus where the Lord had written his name in the book of Isaiah, 175 years before he was even born.

Daniel revealed through G-d's word His plan for King Cyrus and for the return of the Jewish people to their homeland after their captivity in Babylon. The Lord would use His angel and the prophet Daniel to thwart the evil plans of the prince of Persia and manifest His eternal prophetic plan for His people.

During the days of Daniel, both Jerusalem and the Temple lay in ruins. Yet 175 years before his birth, the prophet Isaiah had prophesied that a king named Cyrus would arise and that he would set the Jews free from their captivity and allow them to return to rebuild the Temple!

> So said the Lord, your Redeemer, and the One Who formed you from the womb, "I am the Lord Who makes everything, Who stretched forth the heavens alone, Who spread out the earth from My power. Who frustrates the signs of imposters, and diviners He makes mad; He turns the wise backwards, and makes their knowledge foolish. He fulfills the word of His servant, and the counsel of His messenger He completes; Who says of Jerusalem, 'It shall be settled,' and of the cities of Judah, 'They shall be built, and its ruins I will erect.' Who says to the deep, 'Be dry, and I will dry up your rivers.' Who says of Cyrus, 'He is My shepherd, and all My desire he shall fulfill,' and to say of Jerusalem, 'It shall be built, and the Temple shall be founded'" (Isaiah 44:24–28).

We find in the first chapter of the book of Ezra dramatic confirmation of G-d's earlier prophetic word from Isaiah concerning the proclamation issued by King Cyrus, which set the Jews free from their captivity in Babylon and sent them back to rebuild their Temple in Jerusalem.

> And in the first year of Cyrus, the king of Persia, at the completion of the word of the Lord from the mouth of Jeremiah, the Lord aroused the spirit of Cyrus, the king of Persia, and he issued a proclamation throughout his kingdom, and also in writing, saying: "So said Cyrus, the king of Persia, 'All the kingdoms of the earth the Lord G-d of the heavens delivered to me, and He commanded me to build Him a House in Jerusalem, which is in Judea. Who is among you of all His people, may

his G-d be with him, and he may ascend to Jerusalem, which is in Judea, and let him build the House of the Lord, G-d of Israel; He is the G-d Who is in Jerusalem. And whoever remains from all the places where he sojourns, the people of his place shall help him with silver and with gold and with possessions and with cattle, with the donation to the House of G-d, which is in Jerusalem'" (Ezra 1:1–4).

Here we see the fulfillment of prophecy in that the Lord caused King Cyrus to do exactly as He had prophesied through Isaiah. The prince of Persia indeed has power, but the power of the G-d of Israel is far greater, and these prophesies are living proof to this fact.

ALL THE NATIONS WILL GATHER TOGETHER TO MAKE WAR AGAINST JERUSALEM

Behold! A day of the Lord is coming, and your plunder shall be shared within you. And I will gather all the nations to Jerusalem to wage war; and the city shall be captured, and the houses shall be plundered, and the women shall be ravished, and half the city shall go forth into exile—and the rest of the people shall not be cut off from the city. And the Lord shall go forth and wage war with those nations, like the day he waged war on the day of the battle. And on that day His feet shall stand on the Mount of Olives, which is before Jerusalem from the east. And the Mount of Olives shall split in the midst thereof—toward the east and toward the west—a very great valley. And half the mountain shall move to the north, and half of it to the south. And you shall flee to the valley of the mountains, for the valley of the mountains shall reach Azal. And you shall flee as you fled because of the earthquake, in the days of Uzziah the King of Judah. And the Lord, my G-d, shall come; all holy ones with you....The whole earth shall be changed to be like a plain, from the hill of Rimmon in the south of Jerusalem; but it [Jerusalem] will be elevated high and remain in its old place; from the gate of Benjamin to the place of the first gate, until the corner gate, and from the tower of Hananel until the king's wine-cellars. And they shall dwell therein, and there shall be no more destruction; but Jerusalem shall dwell in safety (Zechariah 14:1–5;10–11).

We know the day is coming when the evil king of the Fourth Kingdom will go up onto the Temple Mount to declare himself to be G-d and demand everyone on the earth to worship him alone or be killed. Shortly thereafter he will gather all the nations against Jerusalem for war, and the city will be captured, and its women violated.

However, we then have these awesome words: "Then the Lord will come forth and make war on those nations as He is wont to make war on a day of battle on that day, He will set His feet on the Mount of Olives, near Jerusalem on the east." After three and a half years of the reign of the evil political leader, the Messiah will come and set His feet on the Mount of Olives and destroy the kingdom of the evil one forever.

The Mount of Olives will split from east to west, and one part of the mountain will shift to the north and the other to the south, creating a huge gorge. The geography of Jerusalem and the entire Temple Mount will be forever changed. Why does G-d do this? Because the Lord G-d of Israel must remove every building and structure that exists today on the Temple Mount. He is going to rule and reign from a cleansed and sanctified Temple Mount.

THE LORD FIGHTS FOR JERUSALEM AND JUDGES THOSE WHO CAME AGAINST HIM

And this shall be the plague wherewith the Lord will smite all the nations who besieged Jerusalem; his flesh will waste away while he still stands on his feet; his eyes will waste away in their sockets, and his tongue shall waste away in his mouth. And it will come to pass on that day that there will be great consternation, sent by the Lord upon them; each one shall seize the hand of the other, and his hand shall rise up against the hand of the other. Yea, even Judah will fight against Jerusalem! And the wealth of all the nations round about—gold and silver and apparel—will be gathered in very great abundance. And so will be the plague of the horses, the mules, the camels, the donkeys, and all the animals that are in those camps, similar to this plague (Zechariah 14:12–15).

If ever there was a one-sided battle, this is it. Not only will a great panic from the Lord fall upon all those who come against Jerusalem and the Jewish people, but their flesh shall rot away as they stand on their feet!

Then Judah shall join the fighting in Jerusalem, and the wealth of the nations surrounding Israel will be will be gathered in great abundance by the *people of* Israel. Just as it was prophesied in Obadiah, so it will come to pass.

For the day of the Lord over all the nations is close; as you have done shall be done to you; your recompense shall be returned upon your head. For, as you drank on My Holy Mount, shall all the nations drink constantly, and they shall drink and be stunned, and they shall be as though they were not (Obadiah 1:15–16).

As prophesied by Daniel, Zechariah, Ezekiel, Obadiah, and so many other prophets, the Lord in His anger will someday turn the tables on Israel's oppressors, causing them to drink from the cup of His wrath on the day of His wrath.

THE DAY OF THE LORD

And it shall come to pass on that day that there shall be no light, only disappearing light and thick darkness. And it shall be one day that shall be known to the Lord, neither day nor night; and it shall come to pass that at eventide it shall be light. And it shall come to pass on that day that spring water shall come forth from

Jerusalem; half of it to the eastern sea, and half of it to the western sea; in summer and in winter it shall be. And the Lord shall become King over all the earth; on that day shall the Lord be one, and His name one (Zechariah 14:6–9).

The Tanach is the only book ever written that foretold the future with absolute accuracy. The day of the Lord is coming as surely as day follows night. The nations and peoples who seek the destruction of the Jewish people will in the end be judged and destroyed.

G-d is sovereign, and He does not change. This book was written so you would know that the G-d of Israel is alive today, ruling from Heaven just as in Daniel's day. Because He is the same today as He was yesterday, you can be absolutely certain that every word of G-d will come to pass.

If this is the case, how should you live your life today?

That which caused G-d to bring judgment in the past will certainly cause Him to bring judgment today. His character never changes. Consequently, what He could not overlook in Daniel's day—rejection of Himself and His word—He will not overlook today.

Is there any sin in your life that you must confess and forsake today? What do you believe the consequences will be if you are not willing to do so?

As you read this book, think about what you have learned about G-d and His ways. Know that these words have been written to encourage you to return to Him, with repentance of heart and "with joy to draw water from the fountains of salvation," "the spring of living waters."

And you shall draw water with joy from the fountains of the salvation (Isaiah 12:3).

...the spring of living waters.... (Jeremiah 2:13).

ENDNOTE

1. Alan Cowell, "1,200-year-old Book of Psalms unearthed in Irish Bog," *New York Times*, 26 July 2006. http://www.iht.com/articles/2006/07/26/news/irish.php

Chapter Six

DAMASCUS, A CITY IN RUINS

Behold Damascus shall be removed from [being] *a city,
and it shall be depth of ruins* (Isaiah 17:1).

Israel is G-d's time clock, and the hour hand is moving with
increasing speed as the time of Jacob's distress draws near.
Just as was prophesied by the prophet Zechariah, we will soon
see all the nations of the earth gathering together against Israel and Jerusalem.

Why are the nations aroused against Israel and Jerusalem?
It is because the word of the Lord, written in Isaiah, is coming
to pass:

*For the Lord shall have mercy on Jacob and again
choose Israel, and He shall place them on their soil, and
the strangers shall accompany them and join the House
of Jacob* (Isaiah 14:1).

The time of the physical and spiritual redemption of Israel
and the Jewish people has begun. This fact has been confirmed as the Lord has brought back to Israel millions of Jews
after centuries of dispersion and made them a nation among
nations once again.

The very fact that the nation of Israel exists with Jerusalem as its capital is an affront to the Arab-Muslim nations, to many of the nations that comprise the E.U., and to a large majority of the nations who comprise the United Nations.

In the eyes of the Muslim nations, as well as many non-Muslim countries, the Israelis are guilty of two crimes. The first crime is they are Jewish. Their second crime is that they dared to make a nation for themselves within a small piece of land that represents one-tenth of one percent of the land-mass of the Middle East. Israel's Muslims neighbors want all of the land. They want Jerusalem. They want all of the Jewish people dead and the State of Israel wiped off the map of the world.

The very fact that G-d's prophetic word continues to be ful-filled as He gathers Jews from all over the world to settle in Israel is an affront to the nations. This is why they will soon gather together against Israel to divide her land, to remove her sovereignty over Jerusalem, and in one last attempt seek to nullify G-d's plan for the redemption of Israel and the Jewish people.

ISRAEL BECOMES A NATION

Prophetic events beginning to take place today, as well as in the near future, could not possibly come to pass until the na-tion of Israel was resurrected from the ashes of history. Israel had to become a nation after more than 1,900 years of extinc-tion for the time of Jacob's distress to unfold in all its misery.

> *Now at that time, Michael, the great prince, who stands over the children of your people, will be silent, and it will be a time of distress that never was since a nation existed until that time, and at that time, your people will escape, everyone who is found inscribed in the book* (Daniel 12:1).

Notice in Daniel's prophecy it says, "There will be a time of distress as never was since a nation existed until that time." The Tanach reveals that for this time of great distress to come to pass Israel had to become a nation once again, which occurred in May 1948. Again, the Tanach reveals that this will literally be the greatest time of global upheaval since the establishment of nations on the face of the earth.

> *Who heard* [anything] *like this? Who saw* [anything] *like these? Is a land born in one day? Is a nation born at once, that Zion both experienced birth pangs and bore her children? "Will I bring to the birth stool and not cause to give birth?" says the Lord. "Am I not He who causes to give birth, now should I shut the womb?" says your G-d* (Isaiah 66:8–9).

Here we see "living prophecy," because the rebirth of Israel was prophesied by Isaiah thousands of years before it actually took place. No other nation has ever been completely destroyed, its people physically removed from their land and exiled to live among other nations for more than 1,900 years, and then been miraculously reborn in an instant.

Although this event was prophesied by G-d, and it became a reality, most of Israel's leaders and citizens today do not acknowledge the G-d of Israel as the one who actually caused this unique event to come to pass. Consequently, Israel in the twenty-first century is as godless and unholy a nation as any other on the planet.

However, by the grace of G-d there is a small remnant within Israel that acknowledges their G-d and believes that it was by the power of His hand that Israel was established as a nation. They believe that it was the G-d of Israel who defended and fought for her against overwhelming odds in numerous wars perpetrated by the Arab-Muslim nations. This righteous remnant also believe that with the arrival of the Messiah, Israel will be redeemed and spiritually restored as G-d's holy nation and people.

ISRAEL'S SPIRITUAL REVIVAL

Isaiah gives us a clear picture of this coming spiritual revival as the Tanach declares,

On that day, man shall turn to his Maker, and his eyes shall look to the Holy One of Israel (Isaiah 17:7).

In that day the remnant of Israel will focus their eyes on their G-d, and "their eyes will look to the Holy One of Israel" instead of looking for their security in their gods of gold and silver, as do the Gentile nations.

As events become more and more horrifying, the remnant in Israel will rest secure in the Lord G-d of Israel and His salvation. Their eyes will focus on Him; they will call upon His holy name and eagerly seek to abide in His holy presence. The Lord will be their shield, and they will know His peace within their hearts, despite the insults of the nations.

HISTORICAL DAMASCUS

Part of the process to bring about Israel's spiritual revival will involve the judgment of G-d against Israel because she has forgotten and turned away from her G-d.

For you forgot the G-d of your salvation, and the Rock of your strength you did not remember (Isaiah 17:10).

This process of G-d's judgment on Israel will also involve His wrath against some of her most ardent enemies. His wrath will be poured out in full measure as one of the very significant prophetic events prophesied in the Tanach takes place.

This prophetic event encompasses the complete destruction of the city of Damascus. Three specific prophecies were written about the coming destruction of the city of Damascus (Isaiah 17, Jeremiah 49, and Zechariah 9). These prophecies were written by different men over a span of about 200 years.

The harsh prophecy concerning Damascus; Behold Damascus shall be removed from [being] *a city, and it shall be depth of ruins* (Isaiah 17:1).

Jeremiah's prophecy about Damascus was written during the days of the Babylonians under King Nebuchadnezzar. While Nebuchadnezzar did conquer Damascus in 605 B.C.E., there is no record he ever destroyed it. In fact, there is no record of Damascus having ever been destroyed. Certainly, it was conquered by numerous invading armies, but it was never totally destroyed, ceasing to be a city. Consequently, we know that this prophecy in Isaiah concerns a yet-future event.

DAMASCUS 2007

Today, Damascus has the distinction of being one of the primary terror centers in the world. Hezbollah, Hamas, the Palestinian Islamic Jihad, and the Popular Front for the Liberation of Palestine all have major operations located in Damascus.

Damascus is a den of evil. One constant objective is plotted there daily: how to bring death and destruction to Israel, America, Lebanon, and Iraq. It is a place where the merchants of death breed their special brand of terror and violence and spew it forth all over the planet.

> Iraqi television has broadcast a number of interviews with captured Iraqi terrorists who confirmed that they received training in Syria before being sent back to Iraq to kill Iraqis and Americans. Several of the captured terrorists stated that they had practiced beheadings on animals in Syria so that they would be able to use the technique on human beings in Iraq.[1]

Events over the past two years had not favored Syria's former occupation of Lebanon, and perceived Syrian culpability in the assassination of former Lebanese Prime Minster Rafik Hariri was the eventual catalyst for the removal of its military and intelligence forces out of the country. Since its forced departure, Syria has been actively seeking ways and means of reestablishing its presence and influence within Lebanon.

Syria intends to reestablish control over Lebanon through Hezbollah. In conjunction with Iran, Syria has financed, armed, equipped, trained, and deployed an army of Hezbollah terrorists throughout southern Lebanon. They are literally a state within a state. Although Lebanon is supposedly an independent nation, Hezbollah operates as a separate entity with its own army. This army is under the direct control of Syria and Iran.

Israel and the United States have aligned themselves against Syria, while Russia, America's former nemesis, has aligned itself strongly with Iran and Syria against Israel and America.

IRAN-SYRIA ALLIANCE AND STRATEGY AGAINST ISRAEL

The strategy that the alliance between the Iranians and the Syrians plan to use against Israel has five parts:

- The first part of the strategy against Israel is to put facilities in place within Iran that would enable it to process and produce sufficient quantities of fissionable uranium to build nuclear weapons. These would be mated with missiles capable of hitting Israel, Europe, and eventually the continental United States.

- The second leg of their strategy took place on February 22, 2005, when Iran and Syria announced they would unite against any challenges or threats to their nations' livelihoods, a move that could raise the stakes in the ongoing international dramas involving both countries.[2]

- The third leg of their strategy is for Iran to use its emergent "nuclear capabilities" to threaten and intimidate their neighbors, forcing them to align themselves with Iran and Syria so the price of oil can be influenced, along with their willingness to accept euros rather than dollars as payment for their oil.

- The fourth leg of the strategy is to arm Hezbollah, Hamas, and Syria with enough missiles of every conceivable type, range, and power to completely obliterate Israel's major cities. These missiles would contain warheads with the capacity to deliver conventional high explosives, as well as chemical, biological, or nuclear warheads.

↪ The fifth leg of the strategy is for Syria and Iran to equip Hamas in Gaza with missiles, anti-tank weapons and tons of explosives, and train it to use them, in order to open a third front against Israel when Syria attacks from the north with its army and Lebanon launches thousands of missiles into Israel's northern cities.

Since the start of 2006, Hamas is said to have smuggled into Gaza over 20 tons of explosives, as well as anti-aircraft and anti-tank missiles. According to media reports, Hamas has also assembled an armed military force consisting of 7,500 fighters, which is said to include specialized units such as snipers, missile batteries, and anti-tank troops. As *Yediot Aharonot* military correspondent Alex Fishman recently put it, "The Palestinians are arming themselves to the teeth, building a military force, defensive systems and preparing [Hezbollah-] style surprises."[3] Their strategy was tested in the recent war in Lebanon, where Syrian and Iranian direction and funding allowed Hezbollah to build a vast underground network of tunnels and bunkers for the storing and launching of missiles against Israel.

RUSSIAN-SYRIAN ALLIANCE

In June 2006, the Russian newspaper *Kommersant* unveiled Russian plans to upgrade the servicing station it has maintained since Soviet times at the Syrian port of Tartus. The short-term goal is to enable Russian ships to dock at Tartus, with a view to its transformation into a fully-fledged naval base. *Kommersant*'s unidentified source in the General Staff said the Navy plans eventually to relocate the bulk of the Black Sea Fleet, currently in Sevastopol, to Syria.[4]

Reports were emerging long before the Israeli attacks on Lebanon that Russia had begun work on deepening the Syrian maritime port of Tartus, used by the Soviet Union and later Russia as a supply point since the Cold War, and widening a channel in Latakia, another Syrian port. Both Tartus and Latakia are significant for both Syria and Russia in that they face the outlet of the Ceyhan end—the receiving end—of the Baku-Tbilisi-Ceyhan oil terminal, giving Russia and its partners the ability to disrupt or secure the port and route during the possibility of the eruption of any future war(s).

The Russian expansion of the Tartus would include the installation of an air defense system with an S-300 PMU2 Favorit ballistic missile system that would be a virtual threat to the Ceyhan maritime traffic and the flow of oil and would provide an air defense shield for vital portions of Syria that are strategically important, especially in the event of a war. In essence, Damascus (the Syrian capital) and Syria would be protected from either Israeli or American aerial bombardment. It is clear that the Russian aims in Syria are a symmetrical reaction to American objectives for the Middle East and part of a global chess game.[5]

PROPHESIED CONFLICT LEADING TO WAR

"Syrian President Bashar Al-Assad says his country is prepared for war with Israel and warns that the Golan Heights would be seized by 'Syrian hands.'"[6] It does not take a great deal of imagination to visualize that the day and the hour are coming when there will be a major military conflict between Syria and Israel over the Golan Heights, particularly after this recent statement.

The Lord is setting the stage for the complete destruction of Damascus just as He prophesied through Isaiah. He has led Syria into an alliance against Israel with Iran, whose President has publicly stated that he fully intends to wipe Israel off the map of the world. Psalm 83 prophesied that the Arab-Muslim nations would conspire together and make a covenant against the G-d of Israel and His holy people.

For behold, Your enemies stir, and those who hate You raise their heads. Against Your people they plot cunningly, and they take counsel against Your protected ones. They said, "Come, let us destroy them from [being] *a nation, and the name of Israel will no longer be remembered"* (Psalm 83:3–5).

Consequently, the Lord is going to cause Damascus to perpetrate an action that is so offensive to the G-d of Israel that He will bring about its complete and total destruction.

The harsh prophecy concerning Damascus; Behold Damascus shall be removed from [being] *a city, and it shall be depth of ruins* (Isaiah 17:1).

MOAB LIKE SODOM AND THE AMMONITES LIKE GOMORRAH!

We have seen earlier that Edom and Esau are closely linked to Moab and Ammon in prophecy. The fate of Moab and the Ammonites is clearly prophesied in the book of Zephaniah, along with the reason for their complete destruction.

I heard the taunts of Moab and the jeers of the children of Ammon, who taunted My people, and they aggrandized themselves on their border. Therefore, as I live—says the Lord of Hosts, the G-d of Israel—for Moab shall be like Sodom, and the children of Ammon like Gemorrah; a rattling of nettles, and a salt mine, and desolation forever. The remnant of My people shall plunder them, and the remnant of My nation shall inherit them. They shall have this instead of their haughtiness, for they taunted and aggrandized themselves over the people of the Lord of Hosts. The Lord shall be feared by them, for He weakened all the G-ds of the earth. And every man shall prostrate himself to Him from his place, all the isles of the nations (Zephaniah 2:8–11).

It is very clear why G-d's wrath is poured out in the latter days on Moab and Ammon:

- They have taunted and jeered at the people of the Lord of Hosts.

- They have aggrandized themselves on their border.

⇥ They have acted haughtily against the people of the Lord of Hosts.

Because of their sins against the G-d of Israel, against His people, and against His land and Israel's borders, Moab and Ammon experience G-d's wrath in the latter days just as Damascus does—complete destruction, just as in the days of Sodom and Gomorrah.

DOES ISRAEL HAVE NO SONS OR HEIRS?

In Jeremiah 49, there is further evidence that Ammon (northern Jordan) will experience G-d's wrath at this time.

> *Concerning the children of Ammon. So said the Lord: Has Israel no sons? Has he no heir? Why has Malcam taken possession of Gad, and his people have settled his cities? Therefore, behold days are coming, says the Lord, and I will cause an alarm of war to be heard against Rabbah of the children of Ammon, and it shall become a desolate mound, and its villages shall be burnt with fire, and Israel shall possess those who have possessed their possessions, says the Lord* (Jeremiah 49:1–2).

The Lord poses a question to Israel. "Has Israel no sons? Or has he no heirs? Has Malcam taken possession of Gad and his people settled in his cities?"

The Lord is asking why the sons of Israel have not taken possession of their rightful heritage in Gad and settled in its cities. The Lord then declares, "I will cause an alarm of war to be heard against Rabbah of the sons of Ammon, and it will become a desolate mound!" This is the same fate that Damascus is prophesied to experience.

The Tanach prophesies that Ammon and the other cities of the sons of Ammon will be set on fire for their sins against the G-d of Israel and His people. In the end we see the outcome— "Then Israel shall possess those who have possessed their possessions."

Rebellion against G-d and seeking to possess the land He promised to the Jewish people for themselves are going to bring forth His wrath against Ammon and its cities. Because Damascus, Moab, and Ammon have been guilty of arrogance against the G-d of Israel and His people for centuries, as was prophesied by Isaiah and Zephaniah, the day is coming when the Lord finally says, "Enough, no more!"

IN THAT DAY THE GLORY OF JACOB SHALL FADE

And it shall come to pass on that day, that the glory of Jacob shall become impoverished and the fatness of his flesh shall become emaciated.... On that day, the cities of his strength shall be like the abandonment of the forest and the many branched trees which they abandoned from before the children of Israel, and it became a waste (Isaiah 17:4, 9).

In these verses we see that the glory of Jacob (Israel) will fade, his flesh will become lean, his strong cities will be forsaken places, and the land will be desolation.

At the same time that Damascus and possibly Ammon is being completely destroyed, Israeli cities will experience so much damage they will be like forsaken places. These events portend the coming of a horrendous war in which Israel experiences G-d's judgment, but Damascus and Ammon experience G-d's wrath.

Again we see the reason for G-d's judgment on Israel expressed clearly in this chapter of Isaiah.

For you forgot the G-d of your salvation, and the Rock of your strength you did not remember (Isaiah 17:10).

G-d has poured out His judgment on His people for one specific purpose: to cause them to return to Him because they have forgotten the G-d of their salvation and have not remembered the rock of their strength.

The devastation to Israel's strong cities and land will be so great that it will cause the remnant of His people to cry out and call upon His name. It will cause them to remember the G-d of their salvation and to call upon the rock of their strength in the time of Jacob's distress.

SPIRITUAL REVIVAL

This will bring forth a great spiritual revival in Israel.

On that day, man shall turn to his Maker, and his eyes shall look to the Holy One of Israel. And he shall not turn to the altar of the work of his hands, and what his fingers made he shall not regard, neither the asherim nor the sun-images (Isaiah 17:7–8).

The remnant will focus their eyes and their hearts toward the Holy One of Israel and not look to the work of their hands. They will know that only the Holy One of Israel can save them, redeem them, and restore them and their land from the devastation of the enemy.

THE NATIONS ROAR AGAINST ISRAEL

Woe to a multitude of many peoples, like the roaring of seas they roar; and a rushing of nations, like the rushing of mighty waters they rush (Isaiah 17:12).

It is not difficult to envision a future scenario where Syria seeks to re-conquer the Golan Heights and attacks Israel. Syria would quite possibly be joined in her efforts to destroy Israel by Iran, the Hezbollah in Lebanon, the Palestinians, and possibly Jordan.

Can you imagine the devastation that will be visited upon Israel's strong cities as rockets rain down on Israel from Lebanon to her north, from the Palestinians and Iranians to her east, and from Syria to her northeast? As hundreds of thousands of Israelis are killed and wounded and her strong cities are burning with fire, the situation will quickly become critical even to the point where Israel's very existence is threatened. Perhaps Syria will resort to using chemical or biological weapons, leaving Israel no alternative but to resort to a nuclear response. In an instant Damascus will cease to be a city forever, just as it was prophesied!

THE NATIONS RUSH AGAINST ISRAEL

Woe to a multitude of many peoples, like the roaring of seas they roar; and a rushing of nations, like the rushing of mighty waters they rush. Nations, like the rushing of many waters, they rush, and He shall rebuke them, and he shall flee from afar, and he shall be pursued like the chaff of the mountains before the wind, and like the thistle blossoms before the tempest (Isaiah 17:12–13).

As Israel strikes Damascus and it becomes a heap of rubble, the nations will rage against Israel for daring to defend herself, despite the destruction she has already suffered. They will roar and rush like the roaring of the seas in the midst of a hurricane.

Every possible rebuke will be heaped on Israel for mounting such a massive strike. Israelis will be cursed, boycotted, and reviled by governments and the media worldwide. The Muslim nations will bellow and swear revenge. The UN will convene to impose sanctions on Israel. The E.U. will condemn and revile Israel because she did not willingly go down to death and defeat at the hands of her enemies.

Yet the Lord will act on behalf of His people. He will intervene and rebuke the nations and cause them to flee far away from Israel. Many will experience the wrath of the Lord and flee like whirling dust before a gale.

At eventide, behold there is fright; before morning he is no more. This is the portion of our plunderers and the lot of our spoilers (Isaiah 17:14).

Those who sought to pillage and plunder Israel will believe they are prevailing against her, but as morning dawns, they will be no more! The arm of the Lord will move against them, and as the word of the Lord declares, "Before morning they are no more!"

YOU ARE MY WITNESSES

Those who remain in Israel after these events will be witnesses to the wrath of the G-d of Israel being poured out on Damascus, Ammon, Moab, and Edom. Then all Israel and the nations will know that the G-d of Israel is the One true G-d, and there is no other savior besides Him.

> *"You are My witnesses," says the Lord, "and My servant whom I chose, in order that you know and believe Me, and understand that I am He; before Me no G-d was formed and after Me none shall be. I, I am the Lord, and besides Me there is no Savior. I told and I saved, and I made heard and there was no stranger among you, and you are My witnesses," says the Lord, "and I am G-d. Even before the day I am He, and there is no saving from My hand; I do, and who retracts it?"* (Isaiah 43:10–13)

The Arab-Muslim nations all believe they will one day overpower and destroy Israel. Since the war in Lebanon, they have all been boasting and predicting the demise of the nation of Israel. Like lions circling around a wounded animal, they covenant together to plan the coming attack and destruction upon the Jewish people and nation.

Yet what does the G-d of Israel say? "That you may know and believe Me, and understand that I am He. Before Me there was no god formed, and there will be none after me." Just as the Lord declared from His word spoken through the prophet Isaiah, from the beginning, "I, I am the Lord, and besides Me there is no Savior."

This declaration makes clear that the G-d of Israel is the only true G-d. As Syria launches its attack to destroy Israel, possibly joined by the Arab-Muslim nations, the G-d of Israel will act and destroy those who sought to plunder Israel.

Then they will all know what the Lord has declared from His word from the beginning, "I, I am the Lord, and besides Me there is no Savior." This declaration is absolute, as there is no other savior besides the G-d of Israel. The nations who revile and boast against the G-d of Israel, who make a covenant to destroy His people and seize their lands as a prey, will soon know and believe, "Even before the day I am He, and there is no saving from My hand; I do, and who retracts it?"

ENDNOTES

1. Andrew Cochran, "Syria's History of Terrorism," *Counterterrorism Blog*.
   http://counterterrorismblog.org/2005/03/hearing_on_russiasyria_allianc.php

2. Lisa Porteus, "Iran, Syria Pact Raises Eyebrows," US & World, *FoxNews.com*, 22 February 2005.
   http://www.foxnews.com/story/0,2933,147764,00.html

3. Michel Freund, "Right On: The coming Middle East war," *Jersualem Post*, 18 October 2006.
   http://www.jpost.com/servlet/Satellite?cid=11591934 65378&pagename=JPost%2FJPArticle%2FShowFull

4. Mikhail Barabanov, "Russia in the Mediterranean," *Moscow Defense Brief*.
   http://mdb.cast.ru/mdb/2-2006/item1/item2/?form=print

5. Mahdi Darius Nazemroaya, "Russian Base in Syria, a Symmetrical Strategic Move," *Centre for Research on Globalization*.
   http://www.globalresearch.ca/index.php?context=viewArticle&code=20060728&articleId=2839

6. "Syria President, Assad Threatens War," *NewsMax.com*, 16 August 2006.
   http://www.newsmax.com/archives/ic/2006/8/16/1027 40.shtml?s=lh

Chapter Seven

THESE TWO NATIONS, THESE TWO LANDS: WE SHALL INHERIT IT

Because you said, "The two nations and the two lands will be mine, and we shall inherit it," and the Lord was there... (Ezekiel 35:10).

The Palestinians, who are from Edom (modern day Jordan), are declaring exactly what the prophet Ezekiel prophesied more than 2,600 years ago:

Therefore, as I live, says the Lord G-d, I shall commit [acts] like your wrath and like your [acts of] anger that you did out of your hatred for them, and I shall be known among them when I judge you. And you will know that I am the Lord. I heard all your blasphemies that you said concerning the mountains of Israel, saying, "They have become desolate; they were given to us to devour." You have magnified yourselves against Me with your mouth, and you have multiplied your words against Me; I have heard. So said the Lord G-d: When the whole earth rejoices, I shall make you desolate. As you rejoiced over the inheritance of the house of Israel because it became desolate, so will I do to you; Mount

Seir and all Edom will be desolate, even all of it, and they will know that I am the Lord (Ezekiel 35:11–15).

Written over 2,600 years ago, these verses are full of meaning for today. They clearly describe the "everlasting enmity of Edom" against Israel from the days of Moses to today's declaration of the Palestinians, "The two nations and the two lands will be mine, and we shall inherit it."

They seem to have forgotten the part of the verse that says, "and the Lord was there." Furthermore, the Palestinian sons of Esau and their allies have declared on numerous occasions that once a Palestinian state has been established, they intend to completely destroy what remains of the state of Israel so the name of Israel will be remembered no more.

I HAVE HEARD IT!

The Lord G-d of Israel declares, "You have magnified yourselves against Me with your mouth, and you have multiplied your words against Me; I have heard" (Ezekiel 35:15). The G-d of Israel is the living G-d. He is a G-d who sees, who hears, and who acts against those who speak arrogantly against Him. Woe to those who have everlasting enmity toward the living G-d of Israel and His people!

THE WHOLE EARTH WILL REJOICE

Ask yourself what event could take place that would cause the whole earth to rejoice. How could it be possible for Ezekiel to prophesy an event that would take place thousands of years after he lived and that would cause the whole world to rejoice? He could prophesy this event because the living G-d knows the beginning from the end, and He revealed this to His prophet, Ezekiel.

G-d does not hide His secrets from His prophets. His prophets then reveal them to His people so they know that the prophetic word of G-d is reliable and always comes to pass.

Ezekiel indicates that the nations would rejoice at the desolation of the mountains of Israel, which had been given to them. Whether this "giving over" of the mountains of Israel refers to the creation of a Palestinian state or to the loss of this territory after some future conflict is unclear. However, that the mountains will be given over to Israel's enemies is sure. Because of their hatred and everlasting enmity for Israel, all the nations of the earth will rejoice. However, something awesome is going to take place that will astound the entire world.

The Lord declared, "When the whole earth rejoices, I shall make you desolate. As you rejoiced over the inheritance of the house of Israel because it became desolate, so will I do to you; Mount Seir and all Edom will be desolate, even all of it, and they will know that I am the Lord."

Rejoicing will turn into desolation because the Palestinians and the nations have all mocked the Living G-d of Israel. Then He says, "and they will know that I am the Lord!"

All the people of the earth will know that there is only one G-d, and that it is He who rules and reigns over the nations. All nations and people will come to know that the G-d of Israel is truly G-d and that there is no other on earth or in heaven.

THE LORD WILL DEAL WITH THE "REST OF THE NATIONS WHICH ARE ROUND ABOUT"

Therefore, O mountains of Israel, hearken to the word of the Lord G-d. So said the Lord G-d to the mountains and to the hills, to the streams and to the valleys, to the desolate ruins and to the deserted cities, which became a scorn and a mockery to the remnant of the nations that are around. Therefore, so said the Lord G-d: Surely with the fire of My anger I spoke about the remnant of the nations and about Edom in its entirety, who appointed My land for themselves as an inheritance with the joy of every heart, with disdain of soul, because her expulsion was for plunder (Ezekiel 36:4–5).

Not only is the Lord going to deal with Edom, He is also going to deal with the "remnant of the nations." He is going to judge them for one specific reason: they "appointed My land for themselves as an inheritance with the joy of every heart, with disdain of soul, because her expulsion was for plunder."

Notice the Lord calls the mountains of Israel "My land." The Palestinians and the nations round about, as well as the other nations of the world, do not understand to whom this land really belongs. They believe that they can force Israel to give up her inheritance in what the Lord G-d of Israel declared to be "My land."

Because they have no fear of the living G-d of Israel, they will take possession of it with the joy of every heart, and with disdain of soul they will drive Israel from it, just as an animal of prey would do.

> *Therefore, so said the Lord G-d: I have raised My hand; surely the nations that are around you—they will bear their disgrace* (Ezekiel 36:7).

G-d's wrath will be poured out on the nations that surround Israel to the north, to the east, and to the south. In consideration of what they have sought to do to Israel, surely they will bear their disgrace.

Who are the nations that surround Israel today? The nations who surround Israel today are Egypt, Jordan, Syria, Lebanon, Saudi Arabia, and Iraq. Interestingly, most of these nations joined together to attack Israel in the wars of 1948, 1956, 1967, and 1973.

THERE IS A SIGNIFICANT DIFFERENCE BETWEEN G-D'S JUDGMENT AND G-D'S WRATH

If Israel allows creation of a Palestinian state in the mountains of Israel, she will consequently experience G-d's judgment for her sin of willingly submitting to the will of the nations and giving up her inheritance and birthright. However, the nations that surround her will suffer G-d's wrath.

The purpose of G-d's judgment is to humble His people, to cause them to cry out to Him in repentance for their sins, to return to Him and be saved. He uses judgment to bring about the redemption and restoration of His people. Then, when they have sought the Lord with all their hearts and He removes their sins, He will give them a heart of flesh rather than one of stone. He will write His commandments on hearts of flesh and His people will cry out, "We are your people," and He will answer them saying, "I am your G-d, O Israel."

On the other hand, the purpose of wrath is complete destruction by the hand and will of G-d. Sodom and Gomorrah experienced G-d's wrath. Lot's wife experienced G-d's wrath. The city of Damascus will experience G-d's wrath because it will be a complete desolation, never again to be rebuilt. G-d is not like man, for when He pours out His wrath He does not take prisoners.

ISRAEL RENEWED FOR HIS NAME'S SAKE

Therefore, so said the Lord G-d: I have raised My hand; surely the nations that are around you—they will bear their disgrace. And you, the mountains of Israel, will produce your branches, and you will bear your fruit for My people Israel because they are about to come. For behold I am for you, and I shall turn to you, and you will be tilled and sown. And I shall multiply men upon you, the whole house of Israel in its entirety, and the cities will be settled, and the ruins will be built up (Ezekiel 36:7–10).

G-d says, "Surely the nations which are around you will themselves bear their disgrace." Thus we know with absolute certainty that the wrath of G-d will come upon the nations which are around Israel after they have appropriated the mountains of Israel as their inheritance.

Then the Lord declares, "O mountains of Israel, you will produce your branches, and you will bear your fruit for My people Israel because they are about to come." The Lord is going to bring back His people and plant them on the mountains of Israel forever.

The land will be cultivated and sown once again, and the Lord will multiply men on the mountains of Israel, and all of its cities will be inhabited, and the ruins will be built up. What an astounding promise from G-d to the Jewish people. Only because He humbled them and they then repented and cried out to Him is such a promise possible. This proves His everlasting love for His people and for His holy land.

> *"And I shall multiply upon you man and beast, and they will be fruitful and multiply, and I shall settle you as in your early days, and I shall make you better than your beginnings, and you will know that I am the Lord. And I shall cause man to walk upon you, My people Israel, and they will inherit you, and you will be to them for an inheritance, and you will no longer continue to be bereaved of them." So said the Lord G-d: "Because they say to you, 'You are a devourer of men and you were a bereaver of your nations,' Therefore, you shall no longer devour men, and you shall no longer bereave your nations," says the Lord G-d. "And I shall no longer let you hear the disgrace of the nations; the taunt of the peoples you shall no longer bear, neither shall you bereave your nations any longer," says the Lord G-d* (Ezekiel 36:11–15).

After the Lord has poured out His wrath on those people and nations who had appropriated the mountains of Israel for themselves, we see the restoration of Israel to her birthright in the land. The Tanach says the Lord will cause men—His people Israel—to walk on the mountains and inherit them so that the mountains will become their inheritance.

Here the Lord is very specific in declaring who will inherit the mountains of Israel—"My people Israel!"

The mountains of Israel will no longer be a contention between Israel and the nations, for the G-d of Israel will have decided the issue for all time. The sons of Israel will no longer be devoured there in war and conflict. We know this because the Lord will no longer allow Israel to hear the disgrace or the taunts from the nations.

ONE NATION ON THE MOUNTAINS OF ISRAEL

Say to them, So says the Lord G-d: Behold I will take the stick of Joseph, which is in the hand of Ephraim and the tribes of Israel his companions, and I will place them with him with the stick of Judah, and I will make them into one stick, and they shall become one in My hand. And the sticks upon which you shall write shall be in your hand before their eyes. And say to them, So says the Lord G-d: Behold I will take the children of Israel from among the nations where they have gone, and I will gather them from every side, and I will bring them to their land. And I will make them into one nation in the land upon the mountains of Israel, and one king shall be to them all as a king; and they shall no longer be two nations, neither shall they be divided into two kingdoms anymore. And they shall no longer defile themselves with their idols, with their detestable things, or with all their transgressions, and I will save them from all their habitations in which they have sinned, and I will purify them, and they shall be to Me as a people, and I will be to them as a G-d (Ezekiel 37:19–23).

The Lord G-d of Israel reconfirms what His plan is for the sons of Israel when He says, "I will take the stick of Judah and stick of Joseph and make them one stick in My hand. I will take the sons of Israel from among the nations where they have gone, and I will gather them from every side and bring them into their own land; and I will make them one nation in the land, on the mountains of Israel!" This is G-d's plan and purpose for the sons of Israel, that they should be one nation again planted on the mountains of Israel. We see clearly from G-d's prophetic word that He is still on His throne and has not given it over to Allah, to the nations, to presidents, popes, prime ministers, kings, or princes.

Notice that the words "I will" are used repeatedly in these verses. The Lord wants to leave no doubt that He is the One who is causing all these things to take place. It is only by the strong, outstretched arm of the Lord of Hosts, the Holy One of Israel, that these things will happen. It is solely by the will and spirit of the great "I Am" that every word that has been written by the prophet Ezekiel regarding Israel and the Jewish people will come to pass.

No matter how the nations may seek to divide Israel and take possession of Judea, Samaria, and Jerusalem, only G-d's plan will prevail in the end. There will be one king over Israel, and He will be G-d's Messiah, the One who will deliver all Israel from the dwelling places in which they have sinned. He will cleanse them, and they will be His people, and He will be their G-d! Amen, Amen!

ISRAEL RESTORED FOR G-D'S NAME'S SAKE

Therefore, say to the house of Israel; So says the Lord G-d: Not for your sake do I do this, O house of Israel, but for My Holy Name, which you have profaned among the nations to which they have come. And I will sanctify My great Name, which was profaned among the nations, which you have profaned in their midst; and the nations shall know that I am the Lord—is the declaration of the Lord G-d—when I will be sanctified through you before their eyes. For I will take you from among the nations and gather you from all the countries, and I will bring you to your land. And I will sprinkle clean water upon you, and you will be clean; from all your impurities and from all your abominations will I cleanse you. And I will give you a new heart, and a new spirit will I put within you, and I will take away the heart of stone out of your flesh, and I will give you a heart of flesh. And I will put My spirit within you and bring it about that you will walk in My statutes and you will keep My ordinances and do [them]. Then will you dwell in the land that I gave your fathers, and you will be a people to Me, and I will be to you as a G-d (Ezekiel 36:22–28).

Why did the Lord act to restore Israel to her inheritance? He says, "Not for your sake, O house of Israel, but for My holy name, which you profaned among the nations." The Lord is acting to vindicate His great name, which Israel profaned as she lived scattered among the nations. "Then the nations will know that I am the Lord!"

This single statement has eternal significance and meaning. For the Lord is speaking here to all nations and all people, testifying that the G-d of Israel is the living G-d, and so that all the nations and peoples of the earth will know that He is the Lord and there is no other in heaven or on earth.

G-D PROVES HIMSELF TO BE WHO HE SAID HE WAS FROM THE BEGINNING

The G-d of Israel will completely fulfill His covenant promises to the Jewish people, and the nations of the earth will not be able to deny it.

He simply says the words—"I will."

- I will take you from the nations, gather you from all the lands and bring you into your own land.

- I will sprinkle clean water on you, and you will be clean.

- I will cleanse you from all your impurities and from all your abominations.

- I will give you a new heart.

- I will put a new spirit in you.

- I will remove the heart of stone from your flesh.

- I will give you a heart of flesh.

- I will put My Spirit within you and bring it about that you walk in My statutes.

THEN THE LORD SAYS, "YOU WILL."

- ⇢ You will keep My ordinances and do them.
- ⇢ You will dwell in the land that I gave to your fathers.
- ⇢ You will be a people to Me.

THE FINAL I WILL

"I will be your G-d." *Amen, Amen!*

There is no doubt whose will is in operation here. It is not the will of man, nor is it the will of the nations. It is not the will of Allah, nor the will of any religious order or denomination. It is not the will of any evil ruler or of any elected government.

All of these things will be established by the will and Spirit of the living G-d of Israel.

FOR THE SAKE OF MY GREAT AND HOLY NAME

Not for your sake do I do it, says the Lord G-d, may it be known to you; be ashamed and confounded for your ways, O house of Israel. So says the Lord G-d: On the day that I will have cleansed you from all your iniquities, and I will resettle the cities, and the ruins shall be built up. And the desolate land shall be worked, instead of its lying desolate in the sight of all that pass by. And they shall say, "This land that was desolate has become like the Garden of Eden, and the cities that were destroyed and desolate and pulled down have become settled as fortified [cities]." And the nations that are left round about you shall know that I, the Lord, have built up the ruined places and have planted the desolate ones; I, the Lord, have spoken, and I will perform [it] (Ezekiel 36:32–36).

Here the Lord is rebuking the nation of Israel, its political and religious leaders, its rabbis, prophets, and priests, saying, "Be ashamed and confounded in your ways!" Their ways have been the ways of men, not of G-d. Their ways caused them to sin grievously against G-d. They did not hear His voice, nor did they obey His commandments. They chose to walk in the ways of the world and of men. Be ashamed, you who forsook the rock of your salvation.

Yet, for the sake of His great and holy name G-d says,

- "I will cleanse you from all your iniquities!"

- "I will cause the cities to be resettled and the ruins to be rebuilt."

- "I will cause the desolate land to be worked instead of lying desolate."

- "I will cause people to say, 'The desolate land has become like the Garden of Eden.'"

- "The nations and people round about you will know and understand that I, the Lord, have rebuilt the ruined places and planted that which was desolate."

- "I, the Lord, have spoken, and I will perform it!"

Chapter Eight

GOG AND MAGOG

And Zion said, "The Lord has forsaken me, and the Lord has forgotten me." Shall a woman forget her sucking child, from having mercy on the child of her womb? These too shall forget, but I will not forget you. Behold on [My] hands have I engraved you; your walls are before Me always (Isaiah 49:14–16).

When the vast armies of Gog and Magog come against Israel, it will appear to Israelis and to all the nations that the Lord G-d has forsaken Israel and left her to certain destruction. Like an army of hungry lions the enemy will invade the land of Israel seeking to destroy and plunder. However, few people will understand that it was the G-d of Israel who brought forth Gog and his army from the land of the far north for a specific purpose that never entered the mind of Gog, his followers, or the godless nations who join him.

In the days of Moses the Lord hardened Pharaoh's heart in Egypt, causing him to ask,

"Who is the Lord that I should heed His voice to let Israel out? I do not know the Lord, neither will I let Israel out" (Exodus 5:2).

The Lord hardened Pharaoh's heart so when He later humbled him and his army, all the nations, as well as the fleeing Israelites, would know that it was the Lord G-d of Israel who brought Pharaoh and his army to destruction. The Lord's specific purpose was to magnify Himself in the eyes of Israel and the nations, so there was absolutely no question as to who brought the Israelites out of Egypt, who parted the Red Sea, who led Israel across the sea bed, dry shod, and who caused the waters to cover the army of Egypt forever.

The same biblical principles are going to apply in the coming Gog and Magog battle as they did to Pharaoh and his mighty army. The Lord is going to bring forth Gog and his huge army from the far north against the mountains of Israel for a very specific purpose. His purpose is to ensure that Israel and all the nations will know one immutable fact about the great "I Am," who spoke to Moses and is speaking to us today through the prophet Ezekiel.

> And I will reveal Myself in My greatness and in My holiness and will be recognized in the eyes of many nations, and they will know that I am the Lord (Ezekiel 38:23).

No one knows the exact timing or sequence of the coming prophetic war where Gog and Magog will come against the mountains of Israel. However, there is much that can be written that will give us insight so when this war comes to pass, hearts will not be faint nor spirits crushed. Instead, G-d's faithful will be able to stand firm at the outset of hostilities, secure in the knowledge that G-d has promised a mighty victory that will literally amaze the whole earth.

The coming battle of Gog and Magog is described in detail in chapters 38 and 39 of the book of Ezekiel. This epic battle will be fought and won by the Lord, not the IDF or any other human army. It will result in the total and complete destruction of Gog and his army on the mountains of Israel.

The focus of this great battle of the latter days is on the G-d of Israel, as He magnifies Himself once again before Israel and the nations, revealing His will, His power, His eternal plan and purpose, and His faithfulness to Israel and the Jewish people.

THE GREAT "I AM" DECLARES "I, THE LORD, WILL"

The Lord's will is expressed in Ezekiel 38 and 39 when He uses the specific words "I will."

To Gog the Lord G-d of Israel says:

> "I am against you, O Gog, the Prince of Rosh, Meshech, and Tubal."
> "I will turn you around and lead you on."
> "I will bring you up from the far north."
> "I will bring you against the mountains of Israel"
> (Ezekiel 39:1–2).

There is no doubt from these verses that it is the Lord who is leading and causing Gog to be brought forth from the land of the north. The plan belongs to Him alone, and its purpose is to magnify His name before Israel and the nations at His appointed time.

> Therefore, prophesy, O son of man, and say to Gog, So said the Lord G-d: Surely on that day, when My people dwells securely, you will know. And you will come from your place, from the utmost north, you and many peoples with you, all of them riding horses; a great assembly and a mighty army. And you will ascend upon My people Israel like a cloud to cover the earth; at the end of days it will be, and I shall bring you upon My land in order that the nations recognize Me when I am sanctified through you before their eyes, O Gog (Ezekiel 38:14–16).

Imagine for a moment this mighty army coming against the land of Israel, an army so enormous it will cover the land "like a cloud." It will appear as if Israel is doomed to destruction, just as it had appeared to Pharaoh's army when it had trapped Israel with its back against the sea with nowhere to flee.

Yet the Lord will fight for Israel as He inquires of Gog:

So said the Lord G-d: Are you he about whom I spoke in ancient days through My servants, the prophets of Israel who prophesied in those days many years ago, to bring you upon them (Ezekiel 38:17).

The Lord is asking this question so when Gog arises and comes from the far land of the north with his huge and powerful army, those that are living at that time will be able to know with certainty that the invasion was foretold by G-d's prophet, Ezekiel, centuries before, and the outcome will be exactly as He prophesied in accordance with His divine plan.

ON THAT DAY MY FURY WILL MOUNT UP IN MY ANGER

And it will come to pass on that day, when Gog comes against the land of Israel, declares the Lord G-d, that My blazing indignation will flame in My nostrils. For in My jealousy and in the fire of My wrath I have spoken; Surely there shall be a great noise on that day in the land of Israel. And at My presence, the fishes of the sea and the birds of the heaven and the beasts of the field and all the creeping things that creep upon the earth and all the men who are upon the surface of the earth shall quake, and all the mountains shall be thrown down, and the cliffs shall fall to the ground. And I will call the sword against him upon all My mountains, says the Lord G-d: every man's sword shall be against his brother. And I will judge against him with pestilence and with blood, and rain bringing floods, and great hailstones, fire, and brimstone will I rain down upon him and upon his hordes and upon the many peoples that are with him. And I will reveal Myself in My greatness and in My holiness and will be recognized in the eyes of many nations, and they will know that I am the Lord (Ezekiel 38:18–23).

As Gog's mighty army spreads out covering the mountains of Israel, it will appear that Israel will soon be completely destroyed. Many nations and peoples will rejoice at the impending annihilation of the Jewish state. However, what appeared to be certain victory for the enemies of the G-d of Israel will suddenly be turned into one of the greatest defeats ever prophesied in the Tanach.

The G-d of Israel will fight for His people just as it is written: "The battle is Mine," says the Lord!

The Lord G-d of Israel will arise and mount up in the fury of His anger against Gog and his army. The blazing wrath of the Lord will suddenly go forth, causing a massive earthquake whose epicenter will be on the mountains of Israel. It will be an earthquake that is so powerful that the fish of the sea, the birds of the heavens, the beasts of the field, all the creeping things on the earth, and all the men on the face of the entire planet will shake at His mighty presence.

Mountains, walls, and steep pathways all across the earth will suddenly and inexplicably collapse and fall to the ground. Imagine the impact this colossal event will have on every inhabitant of the earth.

Walls hold back water, and they hold up buildings. They separate people, set borders and boundaries, and sometimes they support bridges. Walls are built to uphold, strengthen, separate, and hide. When they fall and violently collapse through the power of this massive earthquake, hundreds of thousands of people all over the earth will be killed instantly.

On the mountains of Israel, the epicenter of the great earthquake, the shaking will be so great that the mountains will split, causing all the walls to collapse. Giant craters will undoubtedly be opened as the mountains fall and split apart, crushing and killing thousands of Gog's troops in the process. As the blazing wrath of the Lord continues to go forth, He will cause the armies of Gog to turn against one another and fight, as "every man's sword will be against His brother."

Pestilence will break out as torrential rains begin to fall, causing floods and death by drowning all across the mountains of Israel. As in the time of Sodom and Gomorrah, the Lord will rain down giant hailstones, fire, and brimstone on Gog and his forces. Those who came to kill, conquer, destroy, and plunder will be killed and plundered by the power of the G-d of Israel!

As the outcome of this war becomes known throughout the world, all nations will behold the stunning victory and be forced to acknowledge that deliverance on a scale such as this could only have come about by the mighty hand of the G-d of Israel. As the nations and their leaders seek to understand the magnitude of this miraculous victory, many will turn to the Tanach to examine the word of the Lord written thousands of years before regarding the fate of Gog and Magog. It will be plain for them to see and comprehend the striking fulfillment of G-d's specific promise of His protection over Israel along with Gog's complete annihilation. From that time forward, no one will be able to deny the wondrous reality of G-d's eternal covenant relationship with Israel.

As He declared in Ezekiel, "I will magnify Myself, sanctify Myself, and make Myself known in the sight of many nations; and they will know that I am the Lord." In the Talmud, it is written that during the days of the war of Gog and Magog, when the Jewish people say the words written in the Kaddish, "May His great Name be blessed forever and ever," they will believe and know that the Holy One of Israel is the Lord.

THE LORD DECLARES HIS WILL TO THE NATIONS!

"I will magnify Myself."
"I will sanctify Myself."
"I will be known in the eyes of many nations."
"Then they will know that I am the Lord"
(Isaiah 44:6).

All the nations surrounding Israel and those who sought to possess the mountains of Israel will know with absolute certainty it was the Lord G-d of Israel who fought and won this epic battle. They will all know that the G-d of Israel is, "the first and He is the last, and there is no G-d besides Him."

So said the Lord, the King of Israel and his Redeemer the Lord of Hosts, "I am first and I am last, and besides Me there is no G-d" (Isaiah 44:6).

The next "I will," is specifically directed to the Jewish people of Israel. Through this great victory the Lord will make it known to the Jewish people that His name is holy, and that He will never again let His holy name be profaned among the nations.

And I will make known My Holy Name in the midst of My people Israel, and I will no longer cause My Holy Name to be profaned....And the House of Israel will know that I am the Lord their G-d from that day on (Ezekiel 39:7,22).

Never again will the holy name of the G-d of Israel be profaned by the people of Israel; rather, it will be hallowed, revered, worshiped, and praised from this day forth and forevermore.

The last "I will" is addressed to the nations, as they will all know and understand that the Lord G-d of Israel is holy in Israel, that He is G-d, and that there is no other G-d in heaven or on the earth.

...and the nations will know that I, the Lord, am holy in Israel (Ezekiel 39:7).

The victory of the Lord in the epic battle against Gog and Magog will be so complete there will not be a single survivor from the hundreds of thousands who joined themselves to Gog and came against Israel. There will be only corpses piled up all across the mountains of Israel waiting to be devoured by the beasts of the field and birds of the air.

Behold it is coming, and it will be, says the Lord G-d: that is the day whereof I have spoken (Ezekiel 39:8).

And you, son of man, so said the Lord G-d: Say to every winged bird and to every beast of the field, Assemble and come; gather from around My slaughter, which I am slaughtering for you in a great slaughter on the mountains of Israel, and you shall eat flesh and drink blood. The flesh of the mighty you shall eat and the blood of the princes of the earth you shall drink; rams, lambs, he-goats, and bulls, all of them fatlings of Bashan. And you shall eat fat until you are full, and you shall drink blood until you are drunk, from My slaughtering that I have slaughtered for you. And you shall be sated on My table with horses and riders, mighty men and all warriors, says the Lord G-d. And I shall publicize My glory among the nations, and all the nations will see My judgement that I performed and My hand that I place upon them (Ezekiel 39:17–21).

G-d's intervention after the invasion of Gog and Magog turns into a feast for the birds and every beast of the field. It is natural for many unclean birds and animals to be attracted to and feed on dead bodies. G-d may be calling upon the birds and beasts to do just that, to feed upon the slain bodies lying on a battlefield of carnage. G-d employs the birds and beasts not only to feast upon the carnage but as a force symbolic of His army against the enemies of Israel.

There is a considerable scientific support for the presence of the birds in the sky over Israel. Millions of migrating birds cross the skies of Israel twice a year between Asia, Europe and Africa.

The website for the UJC provides some additional details:

Uniquely situated at a strategic migration point, Israel is "home" to an enormous, dramatic migration of hundreds of species of birds twice a year...birds fly from Africa over Eilat—then north through the Negev desert—over the Dead Sea—into the Arava and Jordan valleys—and up through the Galilee on their highway-in-the-air into Europe and Asia...This amazing phenomenon occurs from February through May every spring, and from September through November in the fall. The Hula Valley in northeastern Israel is one of the most important bird watching sites in the Middle East. Enormous flocks of about 390 different bird species fly through an area of about 32 square miles....About 30 raptor species have been spotted...over the years, the Gamla Nature Reserve (located in the southern Golan Heights) has become "vulture heaven!"[1]

Also, it is quite possible that the birds and beasts are part of G-d's judgment and they will be part of the divine intervention that decimates the invading armies during the campaign of Gog and Magog, as well as the divine instrument to feed upon the bodies that G-d has sacrificed for them. In the Levitical law, G-d commands human beings to offer clean animals in sacrifice to G-d, but here we see G-d inviting all kinds of unclean birds and animals (scavengers) to a sacrifice that He pre-arranged, at which the ultimate taboo is violated (the eating of human flesh). G-d refers to this carnage as "My sacrifice" and the mountains of Israel as "My table." His judgment of this feast is on the enemies of Israel, as they are given to the birds and the beasts.

WARS OF G-D AGAINST HIS ENEMIES

G-d's word never changes. Although the exact timing of this future prophetic war is not known for certain, we do know it is not going to take place at the time described in Zechariah 14, when "all the nations" of the earth arise and come against Israel. The war described in Zechariah takes place during the time known as the "day of the Lord," where the specific target of the nations is Jerusalem, not the mountains of Israel.

> *Behold! A day of the Lord is coming, and your plunder shall be shared within you. And I will gather all the nations to Jerusalem to wage war; and the city shall be captured, and the houses shall be plundered, and the women shall be ravished, and half the city shall go forth into exile—and the rest of the people shall not be cut off from the city* (Zechariah 14:1–2).

Rather than bringing "all the nations" against Israel, the Tanach reveals that the battle of Gog and Magog involves a discreet list of nations who join Gog and comprise the vast horde that comes against Israel. Below is the list of the modern-day nations that I seek to identify as participants. This list is open to different interpretations as to the specific identity of some of the nations. Nevertheless, this is the list of my interpretation.

The Nations of Ezekiel 38:16	
The Ancient Nations	**The Modern Nations**
The land of Magog	Russia and the Islamic nations of Central Asia
Meshech	Region around Moscow
Tubal	Siberia
Ethiopia	Ethiopia, Sudan, & Somalia
Put	Libya, Tunisia, Algeria, & Morocco
Gomer	Germany, Austria, and other nations of Eastern Europe
Beth-togarmah	Southeastern Europe—Turkey
"Many peoples with thee"	Various other nations allied to Russia

JEWISH SCHOLARSHIP AND MAGOG

The passages in Ezekiel 38 and 39 have been studied in minute detail for thousands of years by various Jewish sages. Genesis 10 lists Magog as a literal grandson of Noah who ultimately gave birth to a nation. This name "Magog" was well known to every Jew who studied this Genesis passage every year as part of the annual Sabbath reading of the Torah. In his prophecy about the future war, the prophet Ezekiel named "Magog," along with other specific nations such as

Libya, Persia, and Ethiopia. This strongly suggests that Ezekiel expected the name "Magog" would be understood by his Jewish readers to be a real nation, not as an abstract symbol of evil.

This claim was further borne out by Rashi when he wrote that in Hebrew, Magog is preceded by the definite article; therefore, it cannot represent the progenitor of the nation, but must mean the nation itself, or those descended from him or "Magogites."[2]

The first to describe the lifestyle of the Scythian tribes was a Greek researcher, Herodotus, who lived in the fifth century B.C.E. Although he concentrates on the tribes living in modern Ukraine, which he calls Scythians, we may extrapolate his description to people in Kazakhstan, Turkmenistan, Uzbekistan, Tajikistan, Kyrgyzstan, and possibly Mongolia, even though Herodotus usually calls these eastern nomads "Sacae."[3]

The Tanach identifies Gog as being from the land of Magog and the Prince of Rosh, Meshech, and Tubal. There can be little doubt that the land of Magog is present day Russia and that Gog is a great King or leader from Russia.

Son of man, set your face toward Gog, [toward] *the land of Magog, the prince, the head of Meshech and Tubal, and prophesy concerning him* (Ezekiel 38:2).

WHAT NATIONS ARE NOT ON THE LIST AND WHY?

While some may not agree with the identity of all of the nations listed above, a more significant issue we must consider concerns the nations who are not named and do not come against Israel in the war of Gog and Magog. The conspicuous absence of Egypt, Jordan, and Syria from the list of nations who join Gog to come against Israel is truly astounding because these are the nations who attacked Israel in 1948, 1956, 1967, and 1973. Furthermore, Lebanon is not mentioned, and they have been directly involved in two wars against Israel, the first war in the early 1980s and the more recent war launched against Israel in July and August of 2006.

Once again we must ask why these nations are conspicuously absent from the Tanach, which describes Gog and his mighty army coming from the north to destroy Israel. Part of the answer lies in recognizing the direction from which the Lord brings Gog's army to attack Israel—from the land of the north! Absolutely nothing is mentioned in the Tanach about Egypt coming from the south, or Jordan coming from the east, or Syria from the northeast against Israel.

The most likely reason they are not mentioned is that the G-d of Israel has already dealt with them and has poured out His wrath upon them so they are rendered literally incapable of coming against Israel. We know from the Tanach that the Lord is going to deal with Jordan, Egypt, Syria, and Lebanon because of their ancient hatred against His people and His land, and for the centuries they have shed the blood of the innocent in the land of Israel.

As we saw in an earlier chapter in the book, the Tanach prophesies the complete and total destruction of Damascus, the capital of Syria. This event has never taken place in human history, so we know it will take place sometime in the future, and this is the most likely reason why Syria is not a part of Gog's army.

We know from prophecy that Ammon, Moab, and Edom comprise the heart of modern day Jordan, and they are laid waste in the latter days, according to Zephaniah, Ezekiel, and Obadiah. Even though Jordan has a peace treaty with Israel today, the Tanach reveals that this treaty will not hold, and they will be judged because of their ancient hatred against Israel.

Egypt has a peace treaty with Israel as of this writing. It also has one of the strongest and best trained and equipped armies today in the Middle East. Yet, the Tanach reveals they do not participate in this war. Why? Egypt, according to the Tanach, has a very bleak future if they are drawn into any future war with Israel. When the Lord acts to take back the mountains of Israel from the Palestinians, or when war breaks out with Syria, it is quite possible that Egypt could be tempted to join the conflict. The results will be absolutely catastrophic for Egypt.

> *And Egypt shall become desolate, and Edom shall be a desert waste, because of the violence done to the children of Judah, because they shed innocent blood in their land* (Joel 4:19).

Just as the Lord prophesied Edom would become a waste, so shall Egypt become desolate because of its outrage against the people of Judah in whose land they shed the blood of the innocent. Another less likely reason is they are simply unwilling to be a part of this war against Israel for reasons that are unknown at this time.

The last and most significant reason is that the G-d of Israel has purposed to bring Gog from the north for one reason—to position Gog's army on the mountains of Israel so that they will cover them like a cloud. If they came from the south or the east, this might not be the case. The Tanach is very specific in naming the exact location where Gog and his vast army are destroyed—"on the mountains of Israel." Consequently, Gog and his horde must advance from the north, coming down as if through a funnel directly onto the mountains of Israel—exactly where the G-d of Israel prophesied He would position them for complete annihilation by His will and His mighty hand.

THE MOUNTAINS OF ISRAEL

> *And you, Son of man, prophesy about Gog, and say; So says the Lord G-d: Lo! I am against you, O Gog, prince and head of Meshech and Tubal. And I will unbridle and entice you and lead you up from the utmost parts of the north and bring you upon the mountains of Israel. And I will smite the bow out of your left hand and make your arrows fall from your right hand. Upon the mountains of Israel shall you fall, you and all your hordes, and the people that are with you; to the birds of prey, to all the winged creatures and the beasts of the field have I given you to be devoured. Upon the open*

field shall you fall, for I have spoken, says the Lord G-d (Ezekiel 39:1–5).

The Lord prophesied first that He would bring Gog and his horde from "the remotest parts of the north against the mountains of Israel." Second, the Lord prophesied that Gog and his army "will fall on the mountains of Israel, you and all your troops and the peoples who are with you."

On the mountains of Israel one of the greatest slaughters in human history is going to take place as the Lord executes His vengeance upon the nations who sought to plunder and despoil the land of Israel.

> *For so said the Lord G-d: Behold I am here, and I shall search for My flocks and I shall seek them out. As a shepherd seeks out his flock on the day he is among his separated flocks, so will I seek out My flocks, and I will save them from all the places where they have scattered on a cloudy and dark day. I will take them out from among the nations, and I will gather them from the lands and bring them to their land, and I will shepherd them to the mountains of Israel, by the streams and in all the dwellings of the land. On good pasture I will pasture them, and on the mountains of the height of Israel will be their dwelling; there they will lie in a good fold and graze on fat pastureland upon the mountains of Israel. I will pasture My flocks and I will cause them to lie down, says the Lord G-d* (Ezekiel 34:11–15).

It is abundantly clear from the above verses that the ultimate plan of G-d is to gather His people from the nations where they were scattered and to bring them to their own land and to plant them and feed them on the mountains of Israel. It is there, upon the mountains of Israel, that the Lord will feed His flock and lead them to rest.

THE NATIONS WILL SEE G-D'S JUDGMENT

And I shall publicize My glory among the nations, and all the nations will see My judgement that I performed and My hand that I place upon them (Ezekiel 39:21).

An integral part of G-d's plan for the redemption of Israel is to cause the nations to recognize that G-d's wrath came upon them because they entered His land for the purpose of ravaging His people and taking possession of the pastures of G-d. The Lord did not act against these nations until they set their feet on the mountains of Israel. As long as they stay in their place He does not judge them, nor does the fury of His wrath come upon them. Yet, once they set foot on the mountains of Israel, their fate is sealed!

G-d's position is defensive, waiting patiently for Gog and the specific nations who join him to come with their vast armies only to be compressed into a very narrow strip of land that will become a killing field. It is because they will choose to seek to nullify His covenant and to despoil His land and His people that He will arise in the fury of His wrath to destroy them. Only afterwards will those who remain among the nations see His glory, recognize His judgment, and acknowledge that the Lord has never forsaken or abandoned His covenant people.

The Lord will bring all this to pass so the nations will understand that He alone is the Lord. It is in the heart of G-d that the same revelation and understanding come to His covenant people. Consequently, after this great victory and deliverance, the Jewish people will all know that He is their G-d and there is no other.

ENDNOTES

1. "The Early Bird Special," *United Jewish Communities—The Federation of North America*.
   http://www.ujc.org/content_display.html?ArticleID =30579

2. A. J. Rosenburg, *The Book of Ezekiel: A New English Translation of the Text, Rashi and a Commentary Digest*, vol. 2, Press Books of the Prophets (Brooklyn, NY: Judaica Press), 326.

3. Jona Lendering, "Scythians/Sacae," *Livius*.
   http://www.livius.org/sao-sd/scythians/scythians

Chapter Nine

THE DAY OF THE LORD

Gather yourselves together! Yea, gather together, O nation that has no desire, before the decree is born, as chaff that passes..the sun; before the fierce anger of the Lord comes upon you; before the day of the Lord's anger comes upon you. Seek the Lord, all you humble of the earth who executed His judgment; Seek righteousness, seek humility! Perhaps you will be concealed on the day of the Lord's wrath (Zephaniah 2:1–3).

The day of the Lord's anger is about to come upon the earth, and all the humble of the land who have fulfilled His law are commanded to seek the Lord and His righteousness and seek humility. The world today puts virtually no value on righteousness or humility. The world equates humility with weakness. The world values financial success while G-d values righteousness and obedience.

WORLDLY WISDOM VERSUS THE WISDOM OF G-D

Human or worldly wisdom tells you to use what is practical in making your everyday decisions. Yet what does the Lord say about our "common sense?"

There is a way that seems right to a man, but its end is ways of death (Proverbs 14:12).

Seeking righteousness and humility is G-d's way, and it is the way to life. When a sincere person seeks divine wisdom, G-d will often lead him to do things that to the natural mind make absolutely no sense.

The Tanach is living proof of this. For example, if a huge army was advancing against your nation, would you choose to defend yourself by attacking the enemy with your national choir going out before your army, singing praises to G-d? Of course not. Yet this is exactly what G-d told King Jehoshaphat to do, and he was completely victorious.

And he said, "Hearken, all Judeans, inhabitants of Jerusalem, and King Jehoshaphat, so said the Lord to you: You shall not fear, neither shall you be dismayed because of this great multitude, for the war is not yours but G-d's. Tomorrow, descend upon them; behold they are ascending on the ascent to Haziz, and you will find them at the end of the valley, before the desert of Jeruel. It is not for you to fight in this [war]; set yourselves, stand and see the salvation of the Lord with you, O Judah and Jerusalem; fear not and be not dismayed. Tomorrow, go forth before them, and the Lord will be with you." And Jehoshaphat bowed upon his face to the ground, and all the Judeans and the inhabitants of Jerusalem fell before the Lord to prostrate themselves to the Lord. And the Levites of the sons of the Kehathites and of the sons of the Korahites arose to praise the Lord, the G-d of Israel, with an exceedingly loud voice. And they arose early in the morning and went forth to the desert of Tekoa, and when they went forth, Jehoshaphat stood and said, "Hear me, O Judeans and inhabitants of Jerusalem. Believe in the Lord your G-d, and you will be believed; believe in His prophets, and you will prosper." And he took counsel with the people, and he set up singers to the Lord that they should praise the beauty of holiness, when they went out before the advance guard and said, "Give thanks to the Lord, for His kindness is eternal." And at the time they commenced with song and praise, the Lord placed liers-in-wait against the children of Ammon, Moab, and Mount Seir, who were coming to Judah, and they were struck down. And the children of Ammon and Moab rose up against the inhabitants of Mount Seir to destroy and annihilate, and when they finished with the inhabitants of Seir, each one helped his friend to destroy. And the Judeans came upon the place overlooking the desert, and they turned to the multitude, and behold they were corpses falling to the ground, with no survivors (2 Chronicles 20:15–24).

If you were the commander of an army that was seeking to take a city that was surrounded by a massive wall, would you command your army to march around the city seven times and then shout? Yet that is exactly what G-d commanded Joshua to do, and it brought down the walls of Jericho.

And it was on the seventh day, that they rose early at the dawning (of the day), and they circled the city after the same manner seven times; only on that day they circled the city seven times. And it was at the seventh time, the priests blew with the trumpets, and Joshua said to the people, Shout, for the Lord has given you the city. And the city shall be devoted; it, and all that is in it, to the Lord; only Rahab the harlot shall live, she and all that is with her in the house, because she hid the messengers that we sent. And only you keep (yourselves) from the devoted thing, lest you make yourselves condemned when you take of the devoted thing, and make the camp of Israel a ruin, and trouble it. And all the silver and gold, and vessels of copper and iron, are consecrated to the Lord; they shall come into the treasury of the Lord. And the people shouted, and (the priests) blew with the trumpets; and it was when the people heard the sound of the trumpet, that the people shouted with a great shout, and the wall fell down in its place and the people went up into the city, every man opposite him, and they took the city. And they completely destroyed all that was in the city, both man and woman, young and old, and ox, and sheep, and ass, with the edge of the sword (Joshua 6:15–16;20–21).

One reason Israeli leaders did not experience victory in the recent war in Lebanon was because they never sought the divine wisdom of G-d before going into battle. They succumbed to worldly thinking, as they completely ruled out any word from G-d because it simply did not make any sense to them. Consequently, while King Jehoshaphat and Joshua experienced victory, Olmert and his advisors experienced defeat.

SEEKING TO HEAR G-D'S VOICE

Seeking to hear G-d's voice is very much like being on the right television channel. If you are tuned into the wrong channel, you are going to miss hearing His voice. The problem is not with the TV station, for it has been broadcasting continuously. But if you have not tuned into the right channel, you are going to miss not only G-d's voice, but His entire program as well.

G-d has been at work all around Israel's leaders since the day He took them out of Egypt with an outstretched arm. Nothing has changed. He is still broadcasting, but no one is tuning in to His channel, primarily because they don't even believe He exists!

To hear G-d's voice you must decide whether to focus on the messages sent out by the world or those that come from the word of G-d.

And you shall call Me and go and pray to Me, and I will hearken to you. And you will seek Me and find [Me] for you will seek Me with all your heart (Jeremiah 29:12–13).

Not seeking the wisdom and counsel of the Lord has been a fatal mistake that the Jewish people and their leaders have made throughout their entire history. Today, just as in times past, our leaders in Israel are not seeking to hear G-d's voice.

Consequently, they have failed to recognize when G-d was speaking to them through one of His prophets, just as their forefathers did.

This has brought enormous negative consequences on G-d's people because we have missed hearing and responding to His voice. G-d is sovereign, and He does not change. The consequences of past mistakes should be a wake-up call to all Jewish people and to Israel's leaders today.

Consider what G-d said to those who disregarded and despised His word.

> *And the Lord G-d of their forefathers sent upon them through His messengers, sending them early and often, for He had pity on His people and on His abode. But they mocked the messengers of G-d, and despised His words and scoffed His prophets, until the Lord's wrath ascended upon His people beyond remedy* (2 Chronicles 36:15–16).

> *And now, because you have committed all these acts, says the Lord, and I spoke to you, going early and speaking, but you did not hearken, and I called you, but you did not respond. And I will do to the house upon which My name is called, upon which you rely, and to the place that I gave you and your forefathers, as I did to Shiloh. And I will cast you away from My presence as I cast all your brothers, all the seed of Ephraim* (Jeremiah 7:13–15).

> *I, too, will choose their mockeries, and their fears I will bring to them, since I called and no one answered, I spoke and they did not hearken, and they did what was evil in My eyes, and what I did not wish they chose. Hearken to the word of the Lord, who quake at His word, "Your brethren who hate you, who cast you out, said, 'For the sake of my name, the Lord shall be glorified,' but we will see your joy, and they shall be ashamed"* (Isaiah 66:4–5).

Undoubtedly, the greatest reason people miss hearing G-d's voice today is their lack of faith. If you do not believe G-d exists or don't believe G-d speaks to His people today, it is doubtful you will hear His voice or even attempt to do so.

A FAMINE IN THE LAND

Today, there is a famine in the land of Israel. As the Lord said, "there is a famine in the land, not of bread or water, but to hear the word of the Lord."

> Behold, days are coming, says the Lord G-d, and I will send famine into the land, not a famine for bread nor a thirst for water, but to hear the word of the Lord (Amos 8:11).

The generation of Jews that came out of Egypt was unable to enter the land that the G-d of Israel had promised them specifically because of their unbelief. The people of Israel today are unable to possess the land that the G-d of Israel promised them because of unbelief in His covenant promises to them.

Many lack faith because they do not believe that G-d loves them, when in reality He loves them with an everlasting love. His love is particularly great for the remnant who walk in His ways, keep His commandments and seek Him with all their hearts.

> So says the Lord: In the wilderness, the people who had escaped the sword found favor; He [therefore] went to give Israel their resting place. From long ago, the Lord appeared to me; With everlasting love have I loved you; therefore have I drawn you to Me with loving-kindness (Jeremiah 31:1–2).

Israel's leaders do not love the Lord, nor do they seek His wisdom or walk in His ways. They are seeking the wisdom of the world and the approval of nations rather than following the wisdom of G-d and taking hold of His covenant promises. Like

Esau, who agreed to trade his inheritance for a pot of soup, Israel's leaders seek to trade their inheritance for a false peace!

Another reason people miss hearing G-d's voice is that they have absolutely no fear of Him. They simply do not revere Him or His living word. Yet G-d's word admonishes us, saying:

> *The fear of the Lord is the beginning of knowledge; fools despise wisdom and discipline* (Proverbs 1:7).

By this verse alone the Lord calls us a nation of fools because we have despised His wisdom and instruction. This is no small matter in the eyes of the Holy One of Israel.

Our G-d has a message straight from His word, specifically written for those who have no fear of the living G-d.

> *For the conductor, of David; The fool said in his heart, "There is no G-d"; they have dealt corruptly; they have committed abominable deeds; no one does good. The Lord in Heaven looked down upon the sons of men to see whether there is a man of understanding, who seeks the Lord. All have turned away; together they have spoiled; no one does good, not even one* (Psalm 14:1–3).

This is a terrible indictment against those who say in their heart, "There is no G-d." This is highly significant for those of us who are alive today, because we are coming to the "Time of Jacob's Distress," and those who do not know the Lord will not enjoy His peace nor experience His protection and guidance during this time of unprecedented turmoil and suffering. Those who do not know the Lord are going to suffer greatly.

MAKE NO COVENANT WITH THE INHABITANTS OF THE LAND

The Lord tests His people to see where their hearts are, and one of the greatest tests for the nation and people of Israel came after they entered the land promised to them by G-d. The Lord did not allow Israel to conquer all of the nations in the land, and He left some of them there for one specific purpose—to test the hearts to see if they would follow His commandments.

> *Now these are the nations which the Lord left through whom to test Israel, all those that had not known all the wars of Canaan. Only that the generations of the children of Israel should know, to teach them war, just the earlier ones did not know thereof. The five lords of the Philistines, and all the Canaanites, and the Zidonians, and the Hivites that dwelt in Mount Lebanon, from Mount Baal-hermon to the passageway of Hamath* (Judges 3:1–4).

This same situation exists today. He has allowed the Palestinians to remain in the land for one specific purpose—to test the hearts of His people. G-d wanted to see if they would follow His commandments regarding what they were to do and not to do after the rebirth of the nation of Israel in the land He promised them.

G-D'S COMMAND TO ISRAEL

> *And a messenger of the Lord went up from Gilgal to Bochim and said (in G-d's name), "I will take you up from Egypt and I have brought you to the land that I have sworn to your forefathers and I said, 'I will not break my covenant with you forever. And you shall not make a covenant with the inhabitants of this land, their altars you shall smash,' but you have not obeyed Me, what have you done? And I also said, 'I will not drive them out from before you, and they will be pokers to you and their gods will be a stumbling block to you'"* (Judges 2:1–3).

G-d's word is eternal, and His commandments do not change, because He does not change. In the Book of Judges we read how Israel suffered terribly because they turned away and did not follow the two specific commandments the Lord gave to them when they entered the land.

No verses in the entire Tanach reveal more about why modern Israel finds itself in the impossible position it is in today than these verses from Judges. His instructions to ancient Israel were very clear, and they apply to us today as Israel faces the same challenges regarding the inhabitants of the land.

The Lord's commands to Israel:

1. Make no covenant with the inhabitants of this land.

2. Tear down their altars.

In 1967, the Lord gave Israel one of the most astounding military victories in modern times, when Israel defeated the Arab-Muslim armies from Syria, Egypt, and Jordan in just six days. Incredibly, after 1,900 years of exile, the Lord returned to Israel full control over Jerusalem and the Temple Mount. What did Israel do to the altar with the gold dome sitting atop the Temple Mount? Did they tear it down and build a new Temple? No, Israel gave administrative control over the Temple Mount back to the Muslims in direct contradiction to G-d's specific command.

On the issue of not making a covenant with the inhabitants of the land, what has every successive Israeli government sought to do since the early 1990s? They have sought in every possible way to make a covenant with the inhabitants of the land, who call themselves Palestinians!

What kind of covenant have they sought to make with the inhabitants of the land? They have sought to give up control over half of Jerusalem and to cede Judea, Samaria, and Gaza to the worshipers of Islam. Thus yet, to this very day, instead of doing what the Lord G-d of Israel commanded them to do, successive Israeli governments have chosen to do the exact opposite.

The Lord promised blessings to those who chose to follow His commands and curses upon those who chose to disobey His commands. The Lord spoke to all Israel, saying, "Look what you have done!" Today, the bankruptcy of the "peace process" is living testimony that Israel is reaping a terrible harvest because of her disobedience.

Part of the reason that Israel has chosen to turn against their G-d and His commandments is the constant and unrelenting pressure from the nations for them to abandon their G-d and His covenant promises. This is particularly true for America, which has led the Quartet and continues to this very day to cause Israel to give up her inheritance to the worshipers of Islam in order to create a Palestinian state on the very land the Lord promised to Israel.

THE CONSEQUENCES TO THE NATIONS COMING AGAINST ISRAEL: G-D'S CUP OF WRATH

For so said the Lord G-d of Israel to me; Take this cup of the wine of fury from My hand, and you shall give it to all the nations to whom I send you, to drink. And they shall drink and reel to and fro and be like madmen because of the sword that I am sending among them. And I took the cup from the hand of the Lord, and I gave it to all the nations to whom the Lord had sent me, to drink (Jeremiah 25:15–17).

As the great day of the Lord approaches, He is going to send forth His cup of wrath and cause all the nations to drink from it. When they drink of this cup they will go mad because of the sword that the Lord will send among them.

And all the kings of the north, both near and far, one after the other, and all the kingdoms of the earth that are upon the face of the earth; and the king of Sheshach shall drink after them. And you shall say to them: So said the Lord G-d of Israel; Drink, become drunk, and vomit, fall and you shall not rise, because of the sword that I am sending among you. And it shall be, if they refuse to take the cup from your hand to drink, that you shall say to them: So said the Lord of Hosts: You shall surely drink. For behold, with the city upon which My name is called, I commence to bring evil, and shall you be cleared? You shall not be cleared, for I call a sword upon all the inhabitants of the earth, says the Lord of Hosts. And you prophesy to them all these words, and you shall say to them: The Lord shall roar from above, and from His Holy Habitation He shall give forth His voice; He shall roar over His habitation; "Hedad!" He shall call out like those who tread grapes, to all the inhabitants of the earth (Jeremiah 25:26–30).

As the Lord brings the nations against Jerusalem, know He will bring a sword upon all the inhabitants of the earth. Many will seek to do everything in their power to keep from drinking from the Lord's cup of wrath, but the Lord of Hosts says, "You shall surely drink it!" None shall escape.

THE LORD HAS A CONTROVERSY WITH THE NATIONS

A stirring has come until the end of the earth, for G-d has a controversy with the nations; He contends with all flesh. The wicked He has delivered to the sword, says the Lord. So said the Lord of Hosts: Behold evil goes forth from nation to nation, and a great storm shall be awakened from the ends of the earth. And those slain by the Lord shall be on that day from the end of the earth to the end of the earth; they shall not be lamented; neither gathered nor buried. They shall be as dung on the face of the earth (Jeremiah 25:31–33).

The whole earth will shake and tremble as the Lord enters into judgment with all flesh. The wicked will be given over to the sword. Violence and death will stalk the inhabitants of the earth as never before, and none of the wicked shall escape. Those slain by the Lord shall be from one end of the earth to the other, and none shall escape. No, not one!

THE LORD COMFORTS AND PROTECTS HIS PEOPLE

Hearken to Me, you pursuers of righteousness, you seekers of the Lord; look at the rock whence you were hewn and at the hole of the pit whence you were dug. Look at Abraham your father and at Sarah who bore you, for when he was but one I called him, and I blessed him and made him many. For the Lord shall console Zion, He shall console all its ruins, and He shall make its desert like a paradise and its wasteland like the garden of the Lord; joy and happiness shall be found therein, thanksgiving and a voice of song....

I, yea I am He Who consoles you; who are you that you fear man who will die and the son of man, who shall be made [as] grass?

Therefore, hearken now to this, you poor one, and who is drunk but not from wine. So said your Master, the Lord, and your G-d Who shall judge His people, "Behold, I took from you the cup of weakness; the dregs of the cup of My wrath—you shall no longer continue to drink it. And I will place it into the hand of those who cause you to wander, who said to your soul, 'Bend down and let us cross,' and you made your body like the earth and like the street for those who cross" (Isaiah 51:1–3;12;21–23).

In the latter days, the Lord will take the cup of wrath and weakness from which Israel has been continually forced to drink and put it into the hands of her tormentors, the nations.

Never again will the Jewish people drink from the Lord's cup of wrath. They will dwell safely forever under the shadow of His wings. They will be His people and He will be their G-d!

THE GREAT DAY OF THE LORD IS APPROACHING

The great day of the Lord is near; it is near and hastens greatly, the sound of the day of the Lord, wherein the mighty man cries bitterly. That day is a day of wrath; a day of trouble and distress; a day of ruin and desolation; a day of darkness and gloom; a day of clouds and thick darkness; a day of shofar and alarm against the fortified cities and against the high towers. And I will bring distress upon men, and they shall walk like the blind, for they have sinned against the Lord. And their blood shall be shed like dust, and their flesh like dung. Neither their silver nor their gold will be able to save them on the day of the Lord's wrath. And with the fire of His passion the entire land shall be consumed; for an end, yea, a sudden end, He shall make of all the inhabitants of the land (Zephaniah 1:14–18).

We wrote about the cup of the Lord's wrath being drunk by all the nations of the earth. The day in which they shall drink of this cup is called the "Great Day of the Lord" or the "Time of Jacob's Distress."

The "Great Day of the Lord," is a day described by the prophet Zephaniah as a time of trouble and distress, ruin and desolation, of darkness and deep gloom, when the Lord will bring distress on the people who have sinned against Him.

Their silver and gold shall not avail them salvation on that day. It is a day that shall encompass the entire earth with G-d's fearsome wrath. It is a day when the Lord will judge the nations and peoples who forced Israel to divide up His land among them. It is a day when the Lord will judge the nations who came against Jerusalem and Judah to destroy them, and give them over to a foreign god.

Lament, for the day of the Lord is near; like a raid from the Almighty it shall come. Therefore, all hands shall grow feeble, and the heart of every mortal shall melt. And they shall panic; pangs and throes shall seize them; like a woman in confinement they shall writhe; each man shall be amazed at his fellow; their faces are faces of flames. Behold, the day of the Lord is coming, cruel with wrath and burning anger, to make the land desolate, and its sinners He shall destroy from it (Isaiah 13:6–9).

The day of the Lord is a day of wailing and destruction that comes upon the earth by the hand of the Almighty. It is a day that will be cruel, filled with the fury of the Lord and His burning anger against those who have sinned against Him.

It will be a day when every man's heart will melt in fear and be terrified as the fury of the Lord is poured out upon man.

There will be nowhere to hide, as none will escape the day of the Lord.

THE LORD WILL SHAKE THE HEAVENS AND THE EARTH

For the stars of the heavens and its constellations shall not allow their light to illuminate, the sun has become dark in its going forth, and the moon shall not shine its light. And I will visit evil upon the earth, and upon the wicked their iniquity; and I will cut off the pride of the presumptuous, and the arrogance of the tyrants I will humble. I will make mortal man dearer than fine gold, and man [dearer] than the collection of the gold of Ophir. Therefore, I will make heaven quake, and the earth will quake out of its place, because of the anger of the Lord of Hosts, and on the day of His burning wrath (Isaiah 13:10–13).

On this day the stars of the heavens will not shine nor give forth their light, and when the sun rises in the morning it will be dark, and at night the moon will shed no light. Can you imagine a time when there is nothing but darkness? It will be a terrifying day.

Not only will there be oppressive darkness, but the Lord will make the heavens tremble, and the earth will be shaken from its place, experiencing huge earthquakes and shakings as the fury of the Lord of hosts goes forth against the world for its evil against Him and His holy people.

The proud, the ruthless, and the arrogant who have reviled the Lord and mocked His word and His covenant with His people will come to their end, and mortal man will become scarcer than pure gold. This is the day when the Lord will bring judgment upon the earth, the heavens, the people and the nations for their arrogance and sins against Him, against Israel, against Jerusalem, and against His holy people. No one will escape His day of wrath.

THE NATIONS GATHER TOGETHER TO DIVIDE UP G-D'S LAND

One does not have to be a prophet to recognize that all of the nations of the earth are aligning themselves against Israel, seeking to force her to give over her inheritance in the land and her sovereignty over Jerusalem to the nations who worship foreign gods.

As relentlessly as the nations are seeking to bring this to pass, so is the day of the Lord's wrath coming to judge them for their actions against the G-d of Israel, His people and against His land.

> *I will gather all the nations and I will take them down to the Valley of Jehoshaphat, and I will contend with them there concerning My people and My heritage, Israel, which they scattered among the nations, and My land they divided (Joel 4:2).*

The Lord speaks and says that this is the day spoken of by the prophets when He will gather all the nations and bring them down to the Valley of Jehoshaphat in order to judge them for what they have done to His land and His very own people—Israel!

What did all the nations do to cause all this to take place? The Lord says, "They divided My land."

THE WINEPRESS OF G-D IS FULL

> *The nations shall be aroused and shall go up to the Valley of Jehoshaphat, for there I will sit to judge all the nations from around. Stretch out a sickle, for the harvest is ripe; come, press, for the winepress is full; the vats roar, for their evil is great. Multitudes [upon] multitudes in the valley of decision, for the day of the Lord is near in the valley of decision (Joel 4:12–14).*

In this prophetic scene, all the nations are gathered into the Valley of Jehoshaphat, where the Lord will sit in judgment. His word says, "Stretch out a sickle, for the harvest is ripe;

come, press, for the winepress is full and the vats roar, for their evil is great."

So much blood is going to flow that the entire valley of decision will be overflowing from the multitudes of the slain on the day of the Lord. Just as grapes are pressed in a winepress until the pressure on them causes them to give forth their juices, so will the Lord crush the nations and peoples in the valley of decision, and their blood will pour forth and fill the valley to overflowing. No one will escape the wrath of the Lord in the valley of decision!

G-D'S MESSIAH WILL COME AND TREAD THE WINEPRESS OF G-D!

Who is this coming from Edom, with soiled garments, from Bozrah, this one [Who was] *stately in His apparel, girded with the greatness of His strength? "I speak with righteousness, great to save." Why is Your clothing red, and your attire like* [that of] *one who trod in a wine press? "A wine press I trod alone, and from the peoples, none was with Me; and I trod them with My wrath, and I trampled them with My fury, and their life blood sprinkled on My garments, and all My clothing I soiled. For a day of vengeance was in My heart, and the year of My redemption has arrived. And I looked and there was no one helping, and I was astounded and there was no one supporting, and My arm saved for Me, and My fury—that supported Me. And I trod peoples with My wrath, and I intoxicated them with My fury, and I brought their power down to the earth"* (Isaiah 63:1–6).

The Tanach asks the question, "Who is this coming from Edom in soiled red garments from Bozrah?" It is the Lord's Messiah who is coming straight up through the valley of decision, pressing forward in His great might.

Then comes the question, "Why is Your clothing red, and Your garments like Him who treads grapes?" The Messiah's garments are red with the blood of those whom He will tread down in His anger and trample in His rage, just as it was prophesied in Joel and Isaiah.

He says, "Their life-blood sprinkled on My garments and all My clothing was stained, for I had planned a day of vengeance and My year of redemption has arrived!"

The prophetic words that are written here are terrifying for those who have defiled and sinned against the living G-d of Israel. "I trod peoples with My wrath, and I intoxicated them with My fury, and I brought their power down to the earth."

This is what G-d's wrath will be like on the day He brings the nations and peoples into the valley of decision: no prisoners and no survivors! Yet what will be the fate of the faithful remnant that has remained true to the living G-d of Israel?

And I will perform signs in the heavens and on the earth: Blood, fire, and pillars of smoke. The sun shall turn to darkness, and the moon to blood, prior to the coming of the great and awesome day of the Lord. And it shall come to pass that whoever shall call in the name of the Lord shall be delivered, for on Mount Zion and in Jerusalem there shall be a deliverance, as the Lord said, and among the survivors whom the Lord invites (Joel 3:3–5).

There is a way of escape for those who invoke the name of the Lord. All those who know, believe, and call upon the name of the G-d of Israel will be saved!

I WILL BY NO MEANS LEAVE YOU UNPUNISHED

Ho! For that day is great, with none like it, and it is a time of distress for Jacob, through which he shall be saved. And it shall be on that day, says the Lord of Hosts, [that] I will break his yoke off your neck, and I will break your thongs, and strangers shall no longer enslave them. And they shall serve the Lord their G-d and David their king, whom I will set up for them. And you, fear not, My servant Jacob, says the Lord, and do not be dismayed, O Israel, for behold I save you from afar and your seed from the land of their captivity, and

Jacob shall again be silent and at ease, and no one will frighten them. For I am with you, says the Lord, to save you, for I will make an end of all the nations where I dispersed you, but of you I will not make an end, but I will chasten you in measure, and I will not completely destroy you (Jeremiah 30:7–11).

G-d never contradicts Himself, nor does He make things up as He goes along. He knows exactly where He is seeking to lead His people. Whatever He is doing today will be based upon what He did yesterday, confirmed by His word.

History is important, but sadly, Israel's leaders and people continue to ignore what is written plainly in their own book. The Lord is not going to leave Israel unpunished; yet in His infinite mercy He declares, "I am with you to save you, and I will make an end of all the nations where I dispersed you. However, of you I will not make an end, but I will chasten you in measure, and I will not completely destroy you!" G-d will preserve, protect, and bless His remaining remnant.

LIFE CHOICES

And you shall call Me and go and pray to Me, and I will hearken to you. And you will seek Me and find [Me] for you will seek Me with all your heart (Jeremiah 29:12–13).

The depth of your relationship with G-d is directly proportional to the zeal you exhibit in seeking Him and His truth for your life, as found in His word. If you are not seeking G-d daily, or are doing so in an inconsistent manner, you cannot expect to hear His voice, nor can you expect Him to save you in the day of Jacob's distress.

However, if you call upon Him and pray to Him, the Lord promises He will listen to you when you seek Him with all your heart. This is not an idle promise but something that comes from the very heart of G-d Himself.

The Lord has used me to present you the wisdom of G-d and insight into events that are about to come upon all the inhabitants of the earth. No one will escape them. G-d is inviting you to go into a deeper personal relationship with Him so you will know Him, and will know His voice whenever He speaks to you.

WHOSE VOICE ARE YOU LISTENING TO?

Do you want to know if the voice you are listening to is G-d's voice or your own? Psalm 119:105 gives you the clear answer in that it calls G-d's word "a lamp to my feet and a light to my path." If you search the Tanach, you will find specific passages and verses that will help you make life choices based upon G-d's wisdom, not human wisdom.

This book was written to encourage you to turn and to seek the G-d of Abraham, Isaac, and Jacob—the one true, living G-d—with all your heart, soul, and strength, so you will not be deceived by the voices from the world nor seduced by the great deception that is sweeping across our planet. You must be able to discern the difference between the world's voice and G-d's voice!

The world's voice says, "Be successful"; the Lord's voice says, "Be humble and obedient." The world's voice says, "Look to your leaders for answers and solutions to your problems, or even to yourself"; the Lord's voice says, "Look to Me. Pray to Me and search My word, and there you will find truth, peace, and life." The world's voice says, "Live for personal excitement and pleasure," but in the end that is the way that leads only to emptiness and death.

Because there is no fear of the living G-d, mankind has lost its fear of sin against the G-d of Israel. Few believe there will be a "Day of the Lord," when He will judge the nations, the people, the heavens and the earth for their sins against Him, His holy people, His holy land and His holy city Jerusalem.

Know that "the day" is coming, and nothing will stop it. Will you be one who is part of the remnant who survives this terrible day? Will you be one who will call upon the name of the Lord and be saved?

The sun shall turn to darkness, and the moon to blood, prior to the coming of the great and awesome day of the Lord. And it shall come to pass that whoever shall call in the name of the Lord shall be delivered, for on Mount Zion and in Jerusalem there shall be a deliverance, as the Lord said, and among the survivors whom the Lord invites (Joel 3:4–5).

Chapter Ten

A TIME OF DISTRESS FOR JACOB

Ho! For that day is great, with none like it, and it is a time of distress for Jacob, through which he shall be saved (Jeremiah 30:7).

Now at that time, Michael, the great prince, who stands over the children of your people, will be silent, and it will be a time of distress that never was since a nation existed until that time, and at that time, your people will escape, everyone who is found inscribed in the book (Daniel 12:1).

When the evil political leader of the Fourth Kingdom confirms a seven-year treaty (covenant) with "the many," it will herald the coming time of Jacob's distress. The many include the leaders and people of Israel and the nations. This treaty will appear to bring a genuine peace when in reality it will be a false peace.

A COVENANT WITH THE MANY

And he shall make a strong covenant with many for one week: and during half of the week he shall cause the sacrifice and the offering to cease: and upon the wing

of abominations shall come one who makes desolate,
until the decreed destruction is poured out on the deso-
lator (Daniel 9:27).[1]

In reality, this false peace treaty will be a covenant with death and a pact with hell! The evil leader who makes the covenant will be filled with deception, and his true intentions will be masked by smooth words. The covenant will be very pleasing and tempting to Jewish political leaders because it will promise the one thing that has eluded them since the foundation of the state of Israel—peace.

Above all else, the Jewish people crave peace. Modern history is replete with examples of how Israelis have been willing to trade their inheritance in the land for the promise of peace. In July 2000, Israel was willing to give up half of Jerusalem and 90 percent of Judea and Samaria to Yasser Arafat. Fortunately, G-d treated Arafat as He had treated Pharaoh thousands of years before, hardening his heart and causing him to refuse Israel's offer. You see, Arafat's true objective had never been merely the West Bank, but rather all of Israel.

Ariel Sharon perpetuated this self-destructive impulse by forcing a unilateral withdrawal from Gaza and ceding control to Hamas and the Palestinian Authority. The "peace" that followed is today defined by the dozens of Qassam rockets that have daily rained down upon the adjacent Jewish cities and civilians. And under the present leadership, Judea, Samaria, and half of Jerusalem likely remain on the chopping block, despite recent assertions that the unilateral withdrawal has been "shelved."

So, then, if recent history is a guide, when the leader of the Fourth Kingdom affirms the signing of this treaty, Israel will foolishly embrace this covenant with death and pact with hell, believing it will bring peace when in reality it will merely serve to usher in the fullness of Jacob's distress. The one Daniel calls the "king of the fourth kingdom" will bring forth this covenant with death, and many will hail him as the Messiah because he will appear to be one who accomplished that which no one else has ever been able to do—bring peace to Israel and the Middle East.

THE COVENANT WITH DEATH

Therefore, listen to the word of the Lord, men of scorn, allegorists of this people who are in Jerusalem. For you said, "We have made a treaty with death, and with the grave we have set a limit; when an overflowing scourge passes, it shall not come upon us, for we have made lies our shelter and in falsehood have we hidden ourselves" (Isaiah 28:14–15).

Isaiah prophesied regarding this covenant, and his chilling words reinforce Daniel's prophecy regarding its foundation and ultimate purpose—the destruction of the Jewish people and nation.

Isaiah aptly calls this covenant exactly what it is—a treaty with death and the grave, and a pact with hell. It will be conceived in falsehood, and those who bring it forth will have clothed themselves with deception in order to bring it to pass.

Do not be deceived when you see this treaty being brought forth, for it will not usher in a time of peace but rather the most violent and terrible days that Israel, the Jewish people, and the world have ever known.

Nations, come near to hear, and kingdoms, hearken. The earth and the fullness thereof, the world and all its offspring. For the Lord has indignation against all the nations and wrath against all their host. He has destroyed them; He has given them to the slaughter. And their slain ones shall be thrown, and their corpses—their stench shall rise, and mountains shall melt from their blood (Isaiah 34:1–3).

And you prophesy to them all these words, and you shall say to them: The Lord shall roar from above, and from His Holy Habitation He shall give forth His voice; He shall roar over His habitation; "Hedad!" He shall call out like those who tread grapes, to all the inhabitants of the earth. A stirring has come until the end of the earth, for G-d has a controversy with the nations; He contends with all flesh. The wicked He has delivered to the sword, says the Lord. So said the Lord of Hosts: Behold evil goes forth from nation to nation, and a great storm shall be awakened from the ends of the earth. And those slain by the Lord shall be on that day from the end of the earth to the end of the earth; they shall not be lamented; neither gathered nor buried. They shall be as dung on the face of the earth (Jeremiah 25:30–33).

Behold a storm from the Lord has gone forth [with] *fury, yea a settling storm; on the head*[s] *of the wicked it shall rest. The kindling of the Lord's anger shall not return until He has executed it, and until He has fulfilled the plans of His heart. At the end of the days you shall consider it. At that time, says the Lord, I will be the G-d of all the families of Israel, and they shall be My people. So says the Lord: In the wilderness, the people who had escaped the sword found favor; He* [therefore] *went to give Israel their resting place* (Jeremiah 30:23–31:1).

Let there be no doubt—at the time the "covenant with death" is signed, the Lord is going to enter into judgment with all the nations, and He will contend with all flesh.

As the Lord spoke through Jeremiah, once the "covenant with death" is executed and the evil leader begins his reign, destruction will go forth from nation to nation, and a great storm will be awakened from the ends of the earth.

Remember that in the days to come, this man of deception will arise to power on the heels of the ten "kings" or regional leaders spoken of in the seventh chapter of Daniel. He will quickly move to kill or crush three of the leaders, and in so doing will cause the other seven to submit to his authority. For a period of time, he will have power and control over the world's monetary system, the world's political and economic systems, the world's judicial system, and assuredly a vast army, which he will use to impose his will on the all the nations and people of the earth.

G-D'S REMNANT PRESERVED

And it shall come to pass throughout all the land, says the Lord, two parts of it shall be cut off. They shall perish, and the third shall remain therein. And I will bring the third in fire; and I will refine them as one refines silver, and I will test them as one tests gold. He shall call in My name, and I will respond to him. I said, "He is My people"; and he shall say, "The Lord is my G-d" (Zechariah 13:8–9).

That the "time of Jacob's distress" will result in the deaths of fully two-thirds of the Jews then living is a concept virtually unimaginable today. Yet the sinful rebellion and prideful apostasy of the Jewish people is so great that G-d is left with no choice. Daniel confirms the reason for this awful judgment through the vision given him by the Lord:

And I heard the man clad in linen, who was above the waters of the river, and he raised his right hand and his left hand to the heavens, and he swore by the Life of the world, that in the time of [two] times and a half, and when they have ended shattering the strength of the holy people, all these will end (Daniel 12:7).

G-d's program for the smelting and refinement of His remnant will come to an end only when the power (pride, rebellion) of the Jewish (holy) people is finally broken. It will end when the Jewish people, in their day of distress, finally cease looking to the left and to the right in a vain attempt at securing a human solution to their predicament and instead raise their eyes heavenward in humble repentance and collective supplication for G-d's mercy and salvation.

While the chastisement of the Lord is indeed severe, the focus of the Tanach remains on the remnant. Nowhere is it more clearly described that the Lord G-d of Israel will preserve a remnant than in these verses from Zechariah. He says, "One third shall survive, and I will put them into the fire in order to smelt them as one smelts silver and test them as one tests gold."

The purpose of smelting is purification to remove all of the impurities and foreign particles in the gold and silver. The impurities in us are our sins, transgressions, and iniquities. The Lord is going to smelt them out of His remnant so they will be like fine smelted silver and gold. It will be like a pot of smelted silver that is so pure that if you looked down into it you could see your own reflection.

The remnant will invoke His name and He will respond to them declaring, "You are My people" and they will declare, "The Lord is my G-d." This process of refining is G-d's way of bringing His remnant into covenant with Him. Our G-d is a covenant-making and covenant-keeping G-d. He called all Israel to be in covenant with Him forever. This process of refining is described more fully by the prophet Ezekiel.

I WILL BRING YOU INTO THE BOND OF THE COVENANT

As I live, says the Lord G-d, I will not be inquired of by you. But what enters your mind shall not come about, what you say, "Let us be like the nations, like the families of the lands, to serve wood and stone." As I live, says the Lord G-d, surely with a strong hand and with an outstretched arm and with poured out fury, will I reign over you. And I shall take you out of the peoples, and I shall gather you from the lands in which you were scattered, with a strong hand and with an outstretched arm and with poured out fury. And I shall bring you to the wilderness of the peoples, and I shall contend with you there face to face. As I contended with your forefathers in the wilderness of the land of Egypt, so will I contend with you, says the Lord G-d.

And I shall cause you to pass under the rod, and I shall bring you into the transmission of the covenant. And I shall separate from you those who rebel and those who transgress against Me; from the land of their sojournings I shall take them, but to the land of Israel they shall not come, and you will know that I am the Lord (Ezekiel 20:31c–38).

These verses speak of G-d's sovereignty, G-d's refining process, G-d's judgment, G-d's grace, and G-d's ultimate plan for His holy people. His holy plan has always centered on His covenant relationship with His people.

Nowhere else in the Tanach do we find verses that describe what is written by the prophet Ezekiel, when the Lord once again meets with His holy people face to face. In these verses the Lord chooses to use the personal pronoun once again, "I will" (or "I shall"), so there will be no doubt as to who is causing all these events to come to pass. His prophecies uttered thousands of years ago will be perfectly fulfilled in every detail.

Today, as foretold by Ezekiel, Israel is desperately seeking to be like the nations who worship false gods. These nations worship the gods of mammon, power, self, and, most tragically, the wisdom and ways of man rather than of G-d.

In the verses above, the Lord begins by declaring, "As I live," meaning "I am the living G-d; I am the G-d of the living, not of the dead." Elsewhere He declared, "I am the G-d of Abraham, Isaac, and Jacob." Never once did He declare, "I was the G-d of Abraham, Isaac, and Jacob!"

He is the G-d of the living, and Abraham, Isaac, and Jacob are alive in Heaven with Him. That is why He says, "As I live!"

The first "I will" says, "As I live, says the Lord G-d, surely with a strong hand and with an outstretched arm and with poured out fury, will I reign over you."

There is absolutely no doubt as to who will reign over Israel at the time of the end. With a strong hand and an outstretched arm the Lord will establish His rule, and it will come after a time when fury is poured out over the entire planet. Part of His ruling process involves the refining of His remnant, and this refining will include a final worldwide persecution of the Jews, so great and terrible that only one third will survive.

Remember that during the days of Samuel, the Jewish people asked for a king. They had pleaded for one in the days leading up to the time of Saul, when G-d finally relented and granted their request. It cost them dearly because in their hearts they had rejected G-d's leadership, wanting to be "like the nations" rather than a holy nation, a nation of priests ruled by the living G-d of Israel; a nation and a people through whom G-d's purpose could be fulfilled—to be a witness of His holiness to the nations. Israel's history is a living testimony to their unfaithfulness to their G-d and their constant desire to "be like the nations." This is why Israel must be refined like silver and gold, so that they will know and understand that in the end, G-d alone will be their king, and not man!

The second "I will" says, "And I shall take you out of the peoples, and I shall gather you from the lands in which you were scattered, with a strong hand and with an outstretched arm and with poured out fury."

The Lord scattered the Jewish people throughout the nations of the earth for more than 1,900 years before beginning the process of bringing them back into the land that He had chosen for them. This process is still going on today, and it will continue until He has brought them back from all the places wherein He scattered them.

> *"When I return them from the peoples and gather them from the lands of their enemies, I shall be sanctified through them before the eyes of many nations. And they will know that I am the Lord their G-d when I exile them to the nations, and I shall gather them to their land, and I shall no longer leave any of them there. And I shall no longer hide My face from them, for I shall have poured out My spirit upon the House of Israel,"* says the Lord G-d (Ezekiel 39:27–29).

As the process of gathering His people reaches its climax, the earth will be filled with enmity against the Lord and His people. Nevertheless, by the power of His strong hand and outstretched arm, He will bring forth His remnant and gather them together in the land of Israel once again, *no longer leaving any of them there (in exile).*

The third "I will" says, "And I shall bring you to the wilderness of the peoples, and I shall contend with you there face to face. As I contended with your forefathers in the wilderness of the land of Egypt, so will I contend with you, says the Lord G-d."

The "wilderness of the peoples," is a specific place ordained by G-d for the time of Jacob's distress. It is the place of refuge where He will protect, provide for, refine, and purify His people during the time of Jacob's distress. It is the one place on earth where you will want to be if you are Jewish and alive during this time. Nowhere else on earth will there be such a place of refuge like this one ordained by G-d for His remnant. Jeremiah also has verses concerning this prophecy, as seen below.

> So says the Lord: In the wilderness, the people who had escaped the sword found favor; He [therefore] went to give Israel their resting place. From long ago, the Lord appeared to me; With everlasting love have I loved you; therefore have I drawn you to Me with loving-kindness (Jeremiah 31:1–2).

Interestingly, the third "I will" prophesies an event taking place thousands of years after G-d spoke face to face with the people of Israel during the days of Moses. This latter-day event constitutes the second time G-d will meet with His chosen people face to face, just as He did with our fathers in the wilderness after bringing them out of the land of Egypt.

He says clearly, "I shall contend with you there face to face." Can you imagine coming face to face with the G-d of Israel and surviving the encounter as He enters into judgment with you? If you are a part of His holy remnant, not only will you survive, but you will be forgiven, redeemed, cleansed, sanctified, purified, and made Holy for the reason in the fourth "I will."

The fourth "I will" says, "And I shall cause you to pass under the rod, and I shall bring you into the transmission of the covenant."

The entire plan of G-d for the Jewish people is to bring His people into covenant with Him. The G-d of Israel desires His people to have an intimate covenant relationship with Him. He is not a G-d who is far off, but one who is so near we will actually meet him face to face. For those who love Him, this will be an unforgettable experience. All of His remnant will know Him intimately. The remnant will know their G-d, and they will worship Him with all their hearts, all their souls, and all their might.

Just before the time when the remnant meets face to face with their G-d, He will cause them to pass under the shepherd's rod [staff] of His smelting and refinement in order that they be redeemed, cleansed, healed, sanctified, and purified, knowing their Lord and Savior so intimately that they will cry out with joy, declaring, "You are our G-d!" Then He will say to His remnant, "You are My people forever!"

The fifth "I will" says, "And I shall separate from you those who rebel and those who transgress against Me; from the land of their sojournings I shall take them, but to the land of Israel they shall not come, and you will know that I am the Lord."

All those who have rebelled against G-d and transgressed against Him will be removed from the countries wherein they live and never be allowed to enter the land of Israel.

These rebels are the ones spoken of by Daniel, those whose names were not written in the book of remembrance.

> It will be a time of distress that never was since a nation existed until that time, and at that time, your people will escape, everyone who is found inscribed in the book. And many who sleep in the dust of the earth will awaken—these for eternal life, and those for disgrace, for eternal abhorrence (Daniel 12:1–2).

The time of distress prophesied here is the time of Jacob's distress. The verse in Ezekiel is clarified here by Daniel, as he says, "Some will go to eternal life, others to disgrace and eternal abhorrence." Undoubtedly, those who rebel and transgress against G-d will not only be forbidden entrance into the land of Israel, but will also suffer an irreversible fate—eternal disgrace and damnation.

YOUR COVENANT OF DEATH WILL BE ANNULLED

And your treaty with death shall be nullified, and your limit with the grave shall not endure; when an over-flowing scourge passes, you shall be trampled by it (Isaiah 28:18).

Exactly three and a half years after the world ruler demands to be worshiped as G-d in the rebuilt Temple, the Messiah will come to cancel the covenant with death and remove the pact with hell forever. The Messiah will establish His everlasting kingdom, which will never be destroyed.

The rule and reign of the evil leader will come to a startling end after this three-and-a-half-year period, and the Lord G-d of Israel will slay him and consign his body to a flaming torment forever.

> *I was looking until thrones were set up, and the Ancient of Days sat; His raiment was as white as snow, and the hair of His head was like clean wool; His throne was sparks of fire, its wheels were a burning fire. A river of fire was flowing and emerging from before Him; a thousand thousands served Him, and ten thousand ten thousands arose before Him. Justice was established, and the books were opened. I saw then from the sound of the arrogant words that the horn spoke, I looked until the beast was slain, and its body was destroyed and given to a flame of fire* (Daniel 7:9–11).

In this passage Daniel has been taken up to Heaven in a vision wherein he sees the Ancient of Days, the G-d of Israel, seated on His holy throne of sparks of fire, with wheels of burning fire. Daniel is witness to thousands upon thousands serving Him.

Daniel then sees a court set up before the Lord. The books are opened and the charges read. While all this is taking place, Daniel can hear the boastful and arrogant words that the evil king (horn) was speaking against the Holy One of Israel.

Suddenly, Daniel sees that the beast is slain and his body destroyed, cast into the flame of fire. The evil one who spoke out monstrous things against the Most High G-d, who trampled down and crushed the whole earth, who sought to exterminate the Jewish people and to rule forever, was cut down and cast into the flame.

The kingdom of the beast was crushed and destroyed forever because in its place the Lord has purposed to establish His own kingdom, which will be an everlasting kingdom, and He will send forth His Messiah, as King, to rule and reign over all the peoples and nations of the earth.

ONE LIKE A MAN—THE MESSIAH

I saw in the visions of the night, and behold with the clouds of the heaven, one like a man was coming, and he came up to the Ancient of Days and was brought before Him. And He gave him dominion and glory and a kingdom, and all peoples, nations, and tongues shall serve him; his dominion is an eternal dominion, which will not be removed, and his kingdom is one which will not be destroyed (Daniel 7:13–14).

In these prophetic verses Daniel sees One like a man coming with the clouds of heaven, the Messiah, presenting Himself before the Ancient of Days. Here we see one who has the appearance of a man, and Daniel witnesses that the Ancient of Days gives to him dominion, glory, and a kingdom, and all peoples, nations, and tongues shall serve him; his dominion is an eternal dominion, which will not be removed, and his kingdom is one which will not be destroyed.

The One like a man is divine, filled with the Spirit of the G-d of Israel. He has been given everlasting dominion, glory, and power to rule and reign, and all peoples and nations of the earth will serve Him forever.

He shall rule and reign from His throne on the Temple Mount in Jerusalem, and all will come and worship Him from year to year at the Feast of Tabernacles in Jerusalem.

And it will come to pass that everyone left of the nations who came up against Jerusalem will go up from year to year to prostrate himself to the King, the Lord of Hosts, and to celebrate the festival of Tabernacles (Zechariah 14:16).

The city of Jerusalem that satan sought to control through the evil king, and the Temple Mount upon which satan coveted the worship of the world's people, will in the end constitute the exact place where all the peoples and nations will come every year to worship Messiah, the King, the Lord of Hosts.

Son of man, [this is] *the place of My throne and* [this is] *the place of the soles of My feet where I shall dwell in the midst of the Children of Israel forever, and the House of Israel will no longer defile My Holy Name, they and their kings with their harlotry, and with the corpses of their kings in their high places* (Ezekiel 43:7).

Let there be no doubt as to the identity of Him who will rule in greatness of majesty when Jacob's distress has come to an end. Messiah will rule and reign in Jerusalem from the glorious Temple where He will dwell among the sons of Israel forever!

And the Lord shall become King over all the earth; on that day shall the Lord be one, and His name one....And it will come to pass that everyone left of the nations who came up against Jerusalem will go up from year to year to prostrate himself to the King, the Lord of Hosts, and to celebrate the festival of Tabernacles (Zechariah 14:9,16).

In that day, when the Lord will be king over all the earth, His holy remnant, along with any who are left of all the nations, will go up from year to year to worship the King, the Lord of hosts, the Messiah, and to celebrate the Feast of Tabernacles.

IS YOUR NAME INSCRIBED IN THE BOOK?

The Lord is about the business of separating His remnant as we approach the time of Jacob's distress. He is going to use events and circumstances that will have one purpose—to bring everyone to a point of decision. Each will have to make a conscious choice to choose either G-d's way or the world's way.

Your decision will determine if your name is inscribed in G-d's book of remembrance. Your name will either be inscribed in His book of remembrance or it will not. There is absolutely no middle ground here. Your name is either in the book or it is not. You will either be numbered among G-d's remnant or you will not.

G-D'S BOOK OF REMEMBRANCE

Then the G-d-fearing men spoke to one another, and the Lord hearkened and heard it. And a book of remembrance was written before Him for those who feared the Lord and for those who valued His name highly. And they shall be Mine, says the Lord of Hosts, for that day when I make a treasure. And I will have compassion on them as a man has compassion on his son who serves him. And you shall return and discern between the righteous and the wicked, between him who serves G-d and him who has not served Him (Malachi 3:16–18).

The first characteristic of those written in the book of remembrance is that they "feared the Lord." The one thing that is absolutely missing today in Israel is the true "fear of the living G-d." There is no reverential fear that He is G-d, that He is holy, that He is the Creator and covenant maker, and that He watches over Israel to perform His word, which He spoke regarding His people, His land, His covenant, and His Messiah.

When He comes and meets face to face with His remnant, they will know what it means to "fear the Lord." The question for you to answer this hour is, "Do you fear the Lord?"

THOSE WHO FEARED HIM SPOKE TO ONE ANOTHER

The remnant who feared Him "spoke to one another," and the Tanach reveals that "the Lord hearkened and heard it." Then the crucial words are spoken: "A book of remembrance was written before Him for those who feared the Lord and for those who valued His name highly."

Here is the key to making certain your name is written in the book of remembrance—"Those who fear the Lord and who highly value His name." The Lord declares emphatically, "They shall be Mine." Wow! What a statement and revelation. If you want to belong to the Lord and have your name written in His book of life, there should be no doubt as to what you must do. G-d knows your heart, as nothing is hidden from Him. So if your heart is not right, you must go before Him and confess your rebellion and sin against Him.

He will hear you, He will forgive you, He will redeem you, and He will write your name in His book of life if you purpose in your heart to love Him with all your soul, with all your heart, and with all your might. You must seek to walk in His ways, remembering His commandments and doing them.

THE LORD WILL DISCERN BETWEEN THE RIGHTEOUS AND THE WICKED

The Lord says, "That day when I make a treasure. And I will have compassion on them as a man has compassion on his son who serves him. And you shall return and discern between the righteous and the wicked, between him who serves G-d and him who has not served Him."

The Lord declares that when your name is written in His book of life, "[He] will have compassion on [you] as a man has compassion on his son who serves him." Here is the confirmation of salvation, redemption, and protection from the hand of G-d.

He is going to discern between the righteous and the wicked, between the one who serves G-d and the one who does not serve Him. On the day the Lord discerns between the righteous and the wicked where will you find yourself? On the day the Lord discerns between those who serve Him and those who do not, where will you find yourself? Will your name be written in G-d's book of life and remembrance?

THE NEW COVENANT

Behold, days are coming, says the Lord, and I will form a covenant with the house of Israel and with the house of Judah, a new covenant. Not like the covenant that I formed with their forefathers on the day I took them by the hand to take them out of the land of Egypt, that they broke My covenant, although I was a lord over them, says the Lord. For this is the covenant that I will form with the house of Israel after those days, says the Lord: I will place My law in their midst and I will inscribe it upon their hearts, and I will be their G-d and they shall be My people.

And no longer shall one teach his neighbor or [shall] one [teach] his brother, saying, "Know the Lord," for they shall all know Me from their smallest to their greatest, says the Lord, for I will forgive their iniquity and their sin I will no longer remember. So said the Lord, Who gives the sun to illuminate by day, the laws of the moon and the stars to illuminate at night, Who stirs up the sea and its waves roar, the Lord of Hosts is His name (Jeremiah 31:30–34).

ENDNOTE

1. *The Jerusalem Bible* (Jerusalem: Koren Publishers Jerusalem LRD, 2000).

Chapter Eleven

RETURN TO ME

*Return to Him, against Whom you have thought deeply
to turn away, O children of Israel* (Isaiah 31:6).

The heart of G-d has always yearned for the sons of Israel to
return to Him from whom we have become estranged. We
have sinned against our G-d, and because of our sins and iniquities we have become separated from Him, suffering greatly
because of it.

*Behold, the hand of the Lord is not too short to save,
neither is His ear too heavy to hear. But your iniquities
were separating between you and between your G-d,
and your sins have caused [Him] to hide [His] face
from you that He not hear* (Isaiah 59:1–2).

SEEING SIN, TRANSGRESSION, AND INIQUITY
THROUGH G-D'S EYES

The Tanach says our iniquities have made a separation between us and our G-d, and because of our sins He has hidden
his face from us so as not to hear our prayers. There is a significant difference in G-d's eyes between sin, transgression, and

iniquity. All of these have caused a separation between our people and our G-d, from the days of Moses until today.

Sin may also be looked upon as the door, once opened, that can lead us into transgression, which is an act of sin carried out willfully and with foreknowledge.

While sin can be committed unknowingly or unintentionally, transgression occurs when one commits a sin with foreknowledge that the act about to be committed is a sin. Thus a person's will enters the picture when he consciously purposes to transgress against the laws of G-d.

Iniquities, not sin, according to the Tanach, are passed down to the third and fourth generations. The Tanach has many examples of iniquities being passed down from generation to generation, causing sons and grandsons to commit the same sins and transgressions of their forefathers.

Abraham became afraid for his life because Sarah was an exceedingly beautiful woman. Consequently, he chose to ask her to lie to the Egyptians and say that she was his sister.

> Now it came to pass when he drew near to come to Egypt, that he said to Sarai his wife, "Behold now I know that you are a woman of fair appearance. And it will come to pass when the Egyptians see you, that they will say, 'This is his wife,' and they will slay me and let you live. Please say [that] you are my sister, in order that it go well with me because of you, and that my soul may live because of you" (Genesis 12:11–13).

Because Abraham feared man more than he feared G-d at this point in his life, he sinned greatly, and he repeated this very sin again with King Abimelech at a later time. Thus a root of iniquity was formed through sin and transgression, and this root was passed down to Isaac.

We see this same root of iniquity displayed by Isaac when he too claimed that his wife was his sister.

> And Isaac dwelt in Gerar. And the men of the place asked about his wife, and he said, "She is my sister,"

because he was afraid to say, "[She is] my wife," [be-cause he said,] "Lest the men of the place kill me be-cause of Rebecca, for she is of comely appearance" (Genesis 26:6–7).

Iniquities can also take root when sin advances through willful transgression against G-d's law, exemplified when David chose to willfully commit the sin of adultery with Bathsheba. He knew G-d's commandment against adultery, yet he willfully chose to transgress against Him and His law.

The result of the repetition of a sin or transgression is that it will inevitably develop into an iniquitous root over time if the person does not repent and acknowledge his sin and trans-gression before the Lord.

[The Lord] *G-d,…preserving loving kindness for thou-sands, forgiving iniquity and rebellion and sin; yet He does not completely clear* [of sin] *He visits the iniquity of parents on children and children's children, to the third and fourth generations* (Exodus 34:6–7).

KING DAVID'S SIN WITH BATHSHEBA

One of the best examples of the difference between sin, transgression, and iniquity can be seen through Psalm 51, in which the Tanach reveals how G-d caused David to see his in-iquity, sin, and transgression from G-d's perspective.

Psalm 51 is the account of David's heart cry of repentance from his sin against G-d, which is described in 2 Samuel 11:3–26 and 12:7–10. The Tanach tells us that David went up onto his balcony and beheld Bathsheba as she bathed. The sin of lust went from his eyes to his mind to his flesh. From here the doors to transgression were flung wide open.

We know David's lust for Bathsheba led to adultery, and when she became pregnant, and he could no longer cover their sin, David plotted in his heart to cause the murder of her hus-band, Uriah, by the hand of the Ammonites in battle.

The iniquity of immorality that had been passed down to David began ten generations before he was born, as I will explain shortly. This iniquity led to the sin of lust and adultery, which then led to the transgression of premeditated murder.

If the Lord had not sent Nathan to confront King David, saying, "You are the man" (2 Sam. 12:7), David would never have repented. He would have gone through his life, perhaps tormented, yet believing he had successfully hidden his sin and transgression. However, the G-d of Israel is a G-d who sees, hears, and acts. Although He had seen David's sin, He also knew David's heart, and because he is a merciful G-d, He chose to intervene in David's life in order to bring him back into an intimate relationship with Him.

Remember, the child had already been born from this adulterous affair when the Lord sent Nathan to David, so the Lord had given David more than a year to repent.

We know from this Psalm that the Lord knew David's heart and that David had a heart for G-d, but the Lord also knew that David's iniquity had blinded him and hardened his heart. However, the Lord knew that if he confronted David about his sin and iniquity, David would repent and return to Him. This is the kind of person G-d is looking for today.

> *Be gracious to me, O G-d, according to Your kindness; according to Your great mercies, erase my transgressions. Wash me thoroughly of my iniquity, and purify me of my sin. For I know my transgressions, and my sin is always before me. Against You alone have I sinned, and I have done what is evil in Your sight, in order that You be justified in Your conduct, and right in Your judgment. Behold, with iniquity I was formed, and with sin my mother conceived me. Behold, You desired that truth be in the hidden places, and in the concealed part You teach me wisdom* (Psalm 51:3–8).

Only when David begins to face the reality of his sins and iniquity from G-d's perspective does he cry out, "Be gracious to me, O G-d, according to Your kindness."

Think about it for a moment. How would you define mercy? Actually, mercy is G-d withholding from me the punishment I deserve because of my iniquity, sin, or transgression. According to G-d's law, He has the absolute right to render judgment on me immediately. Only His mercy allows Him to restrain His hand of judgment.

What did David deserve for his actions of adultery and premeditated murder? According to the Law, he and Bathsheba deserved immediate death by stoning.

YOU SHALL NOT DIE

However, when David began the process of acknowledging his sin against G-d, the Lord spoke through Nathan and said to David,

Also the Lord has removed your sin; you shall not die (2 Samuel 12:13).

As the fullness of the conviction of his sins swept over him David cried out, "Erase my transgressions, wash me thoroughly of my iniquity, and purify me of my sin."

Notice that David includes all of three of his abominations in his cry for mercy—sin, transgression, and iniquity.

David's sin of lusting after Bathsheba with his eyes led to his desiring her in his heart even though he knew she was Uriah's wife. David knew well G-d's commandments, but his iniquity of immorality blinded him to the consequences.

The door to transgression was opened when he committed the act of adultery with Bathsheba, because he willfully transgressed against the law of G-d: "Thou shall not commit adultery."

His transgression became even greater when it led to the premeditated murder of Uriah at the hand of Israel's enemies. The sin of lust led to the transgression of adultery, which brought about the further transgression of murder! Again David willfully transgressed the law of G-d: "Thou shall not commit murder."

Iniquity, however, was the root cause of David's actions because it had been passed down from one generation to another through his ancestors. Remember that his ancestor Judah had engaged in sexual relations with his daughter-in-law, Tamar. Understand that this was the beginning of the iniquity of immorality that was passed down the generational line to David and which led to adultery, murder, deception, and lies.

David passed this iniquity on to his sons Absalom, Amnon, and Solomon. Absalom had a beautiful sister, also named Tamar, and Amnon loved her. Amnon pretended to be ill and asked that she come and care for him. His lust for her caused him to rape her. Absalom was so incensed when his father David did not avenge this horrible act that he plotted against and later murdered Amnon for his sin against his sister.

Here, we see evidence of the iniquity being passed from David to his sons. The iniquity of immorality led to the lust of Amnon's eyes, which led to the sins and transgressions of incest and rape, which then opened the door to the transgression of murder.

Later, when Absalom rose up against his father and deposed him as King of Israel, he put up a tent in Jerusalem, went into David's concubines, and had sex with them publicly, before all Israel.

Solomon, likewise, inherited this iniquity of immorality, and as a result lusted after women who worshiped foreign gods. He brought idol worship into his kingdom and to his people through his lust for foreign women and their gods, forgetting that the Lord had said, "Thou shall have no other gods before Me."

His iniquity was such an abomination that upon his death the Lord divided the nation of Israel into two kingdoms. Ultimately, this division led to the destruction of both the northern and southern kingdoms.

David finally understood this iniquity when he prayed, "Behold, with iniquity I was formed, and with sin my mother conceived me." David understood his iniquity of immorality had come down through his ancestors and how it had led him to sin against His G-d. Sadly, he would see it manifest itself again in his sons Amnon and Absalom, as well as in the life of King Solomon, with disastrous consequences for the nation and people of Israel.

AGAINST YOU ALONE HAVE I SINNED!

Our G-d is righteous and holy. Every time one of our leaders sins or transgresses against G-d, we give opportunity for the enemies of G-d to blaspheme His holy name. David blasphemed the name of G-d before all Israel when he sinned with Bathsheba and murdered Uriah.

David repented because he had a heart for G-d. However, he did not repent until the Lord sent the prophet Nathan to confront him, saying to David, "You are the man!" It was not until that moment that David began to see his sin from G-d's perspective rather than from his own. This is why David cried out:

> *Erase my transgressions. Wash me thoroughly of my iniquity, and purify me of my sin* (Psalm 51:3–4).

THE SACRIFICES OF G-D

David's heart and spirit were completely shattered and crushed when the Lord opened his heart to see his sins through G-d's eyes.

> *For You do not wish a sacrifice, or I should give it; You do not desire a burnt offering. The sacrifices of G-d are a broken spirit; O G-d, You will not despise a broken and crushed heart* (Psalm 51:18–19).

David acknowledged and confessed his sins against G-d when he said:

> *For I know my transgressions, and my sin is always before me. Against You alone have I sinned, and I have done what is evil in Your sight, in order that You be justified in Your conduct, and right in Your judgment* (Psalm 51:5–6).

David did all these things "in G-d's sight." The Lord was watching and saw everything David did in secret; He then brought it out of the darkness, into His holy light.

Once this happened, David acknowledged his offense, offering no excuses. He only pleaded for mercy and forgiveness. He fully recognized that it did not matter how many bulls or goats he might offer in repentance. He said, "For You do not wish a sacrifice, or I should give it; You do not desire a burnt offering."

He knew that G-d was only interested in his heart, a broken and crushed heart. This is exactly what G-d has always wanted, not only from David but from the all of His people and their leaders as well.

The problem has never been with Israel's burnt offerings and grain offerings, but rather with their stony hearts and their stiff necks! This is why in the latter days the G-d of Heaven must make a new covenant with the house of Israel: He intends to give the faithful remnant hearts of flesh and remove their hearts of stone.

> *For I will take you from among the nations and gather you from all the countries, and I will bring you to your land. And I will sprinkle clean water upon you, and you will be clean; from all your impurities and from all your abominations will I cleanse you. And I will give you a new heart, and a new spirit will I put within you, and I will take away the heart of stone out of your flesh, and I will give you a heart of flesh. And I will put My spirit within you and bring it about that you will walk in My statutes and you will keep My ordinances and do [them]. Then will you dwell in the land that I gave your fathers, and you will be a people to Me, and I will be to you as a G-d* (Ezekiel 36:24–28).

G-d is speaking directly about heart issues here, not about rote prayers or the blood of bulls and goats. These verses speak loudly about G-d's love for His holy people.

These verses foretell a new covenant that our G-d is going to make with us. It has nothing to do with our piety, our daily prayers, our rabbis, our sages, or our prophets. It has to do with only one central issue—the condition of our hearts toward our G-d.

The condition of the hearts in Israel today is deplorable because of one reason—they are like stone, which makes the people deaf to G-d's voice, unwilling to be obedient to His commandments or to believe His covenant promises.

G-d revealed to David the terribly wicked condition of his heart toward Him. David sought a new heart, and that is exactly what all Israel needs to do today.

THE CONSEQUENCES OF INIQUITY, SIN AND TRANSGRESSION

G-d forgave David, and he did not die. However, the consequences of his iniquity, sin, and transgressions were horrendous for the household of David and for Israel as well.

First, G-d said;

And now, the sword shall never depart from your household for ever because you have despised Me and you have taken the wife of Uriah the Hittite to be your wife (2 Samuel 12:10).

Because David had "despised" the Lord, the Lord decreed that the sword would never depart from David's household. G-d preserved David and his kingdom, but at the cost of his son Absalom and the lives of 20,000 Israelis in battle.

Howbeit, because by this deed thou hast given great occasion to the enemies of the Lord to blaspheme, the child also born unto thee shall surely die (2 Samuel 12:14).[1]

The second consequence of David's actions was that G-d ordained the death of the child that was born out of adultery and murder. The Lord would not allow His enemies to blaspheme Him by such an act; thus He took the life of the child born to Bathsheba as an object lesson. G-d would not tolerate willful transgression by the King of Israel without severe consequences to him, his family, and to all Israel.

Why have you despised the word of the Lord, to do what is evil in His eyes? (2 Samuel 12:9)

Israel has suffered so greatly throughout her history because she has seen her iniquities, sins, and transgressions not through the eyes of G-d but rather through the lens of human eyes and human understanding. The Lord is speaking to Israel's leaders today and asking them the same question that Nathan asked King David. "Why have you despised the word of the Lord, to do what is evil in His eyes?"

Why have our leaders and our people turned their backs on our G-d and on His commandments? Why have we forsaken His covenant promises and willingly given up our inheritance in the land He promised us as an everlasting possession? Why have Israel's leaders forgotten the rock of our salvation, the One who fights Israel's battles and the One who delivers us from the hand of our enemies?

Just as the Lord reminded King David of what He had done for him, Israel's leaders need to be reminded as well. When will the people and our leaders recognize the seriousness of our sins against the G-d of Israel that we might repent and return to Him?

CALL TO REPENTANCE FOR OUR PEOPLE

For so said the Lord: A sound of quaking we have heard, fear, and there is no peace. Ask now and see whether a male gives birth. Why have I seen every man [with] his hands on his loins like a woman in confinement, and every face has turned to pallor? Ho! For that day is great, with none like it, and it is a time of distress for Jacob, through which he shall be saved....

For I am with you, says the Lord, to save you, for I will make an end of all the nations where I dispersed you, but of you I will not make an end, but I will chasten you in measure, and I will not completely destroy you.

For so said the Lord: Your injury is painful, your wound grievous. No one deems your wound to be healed, you have no healing medicines. All your lovers have forgotten you, they do not seek you, for I have smitten you with the wound of an enemy, cruel chastisement, for the greatness of your iniquity; your sins are many. Why do you cry about your injury [that] your pain is severe? For the magnitude of your iniquity, [since] your sins are many, I have done these to you....

For I will bring healing to you, and of your wounds I will heal you, says the Lord, for they called you an outcast, that is Zion whom no one seeks out....

And you shall be My people, and I will be your G-d (Jeremiah 30:5–7;11–15;17;22).

We see clearly in Jeremiah that Israel will be chastened in just measure for the greatness of her iniquity and many sins. Throughout the book you are now reading, we have seen verses from both Jeremiah and Daniel that tell us that despite Israel's many sins, a remnant will be saved through this most terrible time yet to come—the time of Jacob's distress!

Like David, G-d's people must cry out, "Create for me a pure heart, O G-d, and renew a steadfast spirit within me." We must cry out, "O Lord give us a new heart." We must pray and cry out as David prayed. We must acknowledge our sins, humble ourselves, and pray, seeking the Lord's face. We must turn from our wicked ways and acknowledge our G-d and return to Him.

Create for me a pure heart, O G-d, and renew a steadfast spirit within me. Do not cast me away from before You, and do not take Your Holy Spirit from me. Restore to me the joy of Your salvation, and let a noble spirit support me (Psalm 51:12–14).

Only when we as a people and a nation respond to G-d with sincere hearts as David and Daniel did will the Lord hear from Heaven and place His Spirit within us.

Daniel, like David, recognized the gravity of the sins of Israel against her G-d. While in captivity in Babylon, Daniel read Jeremiah's writings about the seventy years that the Jewish people were to be in captivity in Babylon. When He realized the time of Israel's captivity was about to come to an end, he sought the Lord in a mighty prayer of intercession, asking that G-d would forgive the great sins of His people.

In the first year of Darius, the son of Ahasuerus of the seed of Media, who was crowned over the kingdom of the Chaldeans. In the first year of his reign, I, Daniel, contemplated the calculations, the number of the years that the word of the Lord had come to Jeremiah the prophet, since the destruction of Jerusalem seventy years. And I turned my face to the Lord G-d to beg with prayer and supplications, with fasting and sackcloth and ashes. And I prayed to the Lord my G-d, and I confessed, and I said, "Please, O Lord, O great and awesome G-d, Who keeps the covenant and the loving-kindness to those who love Him and keep His commandments. We have sinned and have dealt iniquitously; we have dealt wickedly and have rebelled, turning away from Your commandments and from Your ordinances. And we have not obeyed Your servants, the prophets, who spoke in Your name to our kings, our princes, and our forefathers, and to all the people of the land. To You, O Lord, is the righteousness, and to us is the shamefacedness as of this day, to the people of Judah, to the inhabitants of Jerusalem, and to all Israel both near and far, in all the lands to which you have driven them for the treachery that they have perpetrated toward You. O Lord, to us is shamefacedness, to our kings, to our princes, and to our forefathers, who sinned against You. To the Lord our G-d are the mercies and the pardons, for we have rebelled against Him. And we have not hearkened to the voice of the Lord our G-d, to follow His teachings, which He placed before us by the hand of His servants, the prophets. And all Israel have transgressed Your teaching, turning away, not heeding Your voice, and the curse and the oath, which are written

*in the Law of Moses, the servant of G-d, have befallen us,
for we have sinned against Him.*

*"O Lord, according to all Your righteousness, may Your
wrath and Your anger return now...for because of our
sins and because of the iniquities of our forefathers,
Jerusalem and Your people have become a mockery to
all those surrounding us. And now, hearken, O Lord
our G-d, to Your servant's prayer and to his supplications,...for the sake of the Lord. O Lord, incline Your
ear and hearken,...not for our righteousness do we cast
our supplications before You, but for Your great mercies. O Lord, hear; O Lord, forgive; O Lord, hearken and
do, do not delay; for Your sake, my G-d, for Your Name
is called upon Your city and upon Your people"* (Daniel
9:1–11;16–19).

Today, just as in the days of Jeremiah and Daniel, the people of G-d are experiencing greater and greater distress because they are refusing to acknowledge their sins before G-d
and repent.

With Daniel as our example, we offer up the following
prayers and petitions to our merciful G-d:

O Lord, make all of us fully aware of Your holiness
and how greatly we have sinned against You. Lord,
cause us to understand that because we have turned
our backs on You that You have removed Your hand
of protection from us. You have allowed our enemies
to attack us, to mock us, and seek to destroy us because we are a rebellious people. We are children who
refuse to hear the voice of the Lord and to obey the
law of our G-d.

O Lord, above all, like King David, we must cry out,
"Take not thy Holy Spirit from me!" O Lord, pour out
Your Holy Spirit on us and remove from us our hearts
of stone, giving us hearts of flesh in return. Fill us,
lead and guide us, and empower us to believe and

trust in You alone, O G-d. O Lord, sustain us with a willing spirit!

O Lord, write Your commandments on our hearts of flesh so we will know and desire only You. Cause us to understand that only in our returning and rest shall we be saved. In quietness and trust in G-d shall our strength be established.

If we will pray like that sincerely, we can rest assured that G-d will answer.

For so said the Lord G-d, the Holy One of Israel, "With tranquility and restfulness shall you be saved, with quietude and trust shall be your might" (Isaiah 30:15).

Cause us, O Lord, to trust these words:

With everlasting love have I loved you; therefore have I drawn you to Me with loving-kindness (Jeremiah 31:2).

Cause us to obey these words:

"Sing [with] joy and shout at the head of the nations, make it heard, praise, and say, 'O Lord, help Your people, the remnant of Israel!'" (Jeremiah 31:6)

O Israel, know that the Messiah is coming to redeem His remnant and establish His eternal throne on the mountain of His holy city. Do not choose to ignore the words of this book, but pray and seek understanding from the Lord with all your heart, with all your soul, and with all your strength. Will you be one of the redeemed remnant of the Lord?

Is your name written in His book of remembrance?

ENDNOTE

1. *The Holy Scriptures. A Jewish Bible according to the Masoretic Text* (Tel Aviv: "Sinai" Publishing, 1996). The plates of this edition are made from the Jewish Family Bible, London Edition 1881, with the Hebrew and English Text revised by M. Friedlander, Principal, Jews' College, London.

Additional copies of this book and other book
titles from DESTINY IMAGE EUROPE
are available at your local bookstore.

We are adding new titles every month!

To view our complete catalog online, visit us at:
www.eurodestinyimage.com

Send a request for a catalog to:

Via Acquacorrente, 6
65123 - Pescara - ITALY
Tel. +39 085 4716623 - Fax +39 085 4716622

"Changing the world, one book at a time."

Are you an author?

Do you have a "today" G-d-given message?

CONTACT US

We will be happy to review your manuscript
for a possible publication:

publisher@eurodestinyimage.com